THE U.S. NAVAL INSTITUTE ON
NAVAL
TACTICS

U.S. NAVAL INSTITUTE
WHEEL BOOKS

In the U.S. Navy, "Wheel Books" were once found in the uniform pockets of every junior and many senior petty officers. Each small notebook was unique to the Sailor carrying it, but all had in common a collection of data and wisdom that the individual deemed useful in the effective execution of his or her duties. Often used as a substitute for experience among neophytes and as a portable library of reference information for more experienced personnel, those weathered pages contained everything from the time of the next tide, to leadership hints from a respected chief petty officer, to the color coding of the phone-and-distance line used in underway replenishments.

In that same tradition, U.S. Naval Institute Wheel Books provide supplemental information, pragmatic advice, and cogent analysis on topics important to all naval professionals. Drawn from the U.S. Naval Institute's vast archives, the series combines articles from the Institute's flagship publication *Proceedings*, as well as selections from the oral history collection and from Naval Institute Press books, to create unique guides on a wide array of fundamental professional subjects.

THE U.S. NAVAL INSTITUTE ON

NAVAL TACTICS

EDITED BY
CAPT WAYNE P. HUGHES JR., USN (RET.)

NAVAL INSTITUTE PRESS
Annapolis, Maryland

Naval Institute Press
291 Wood Road
Annapolis, MD 21402

Library of Congress Cataloging-in-Publication Data
The U.S. Naval Institute on naval tactics / edited by Wayne P. Hughes.
      pages cm. — (U.S. Naval Institute wheel books)
   Includes index.
   ISBN 978-1-61251-805-3 (pbk. : alk. paper) — ISBN 978-1-61251-891-6 (ebook)
1. Naval tactics. I. Hughes, Wayne P., date, editor.
   V167.U73 2015
   359.4'2—dc23

                                                        2014040285

♾ Print editions meet the requirements of ANSI/NISO z39.48–1992
(Permanence of Paper). Printed in the United States of America.

23 22 21 20 19 18 17 16 15   9 8 7 6 5 4 3 2 1
First printing

CONTENTS

PREFACE

Every naval officer should wish to *comprehend* the characteristic tactical domains introduced in this anthology. But we must not expect every officer to be *skilled in the practice* of them all.

The first vignette exemplifies the tactics of *fleet* actions that were dominant throughout naval history with an imaginary fleet action set in the twenty-first century. Most of the literature of the past has been about fleet battles. Admirals Samuel S. Robison and Giuseppe Fioravanzo wrote histories of tactics through the ages, but these were fleet tactics seen through that single lens. The most intensive period of writing on tactics was in the battleship era, from 1895 to the end of World War I, when better battle tactics were very much an issue among the world's navies. The Naval Institute translated and published French, Italian, and other nations' authors in the *Proceedings*. In 1912 it published an entire book on tactics by then-lieutenant Romeo Bernotti that was rich in quantitative analysis. For example, he employed what we now call mathematical models to aid in understanding the processes of combat. Chapter 7 by then-commander Bradley A. Fiske illustrates the deep study by many naval officers in that Golden Age of tactical thought.

But modern combat is more than fleet actions. It includes submarine and anti-submarine operations, air combat tactics, the vastly different battle tactics of coastal combat, and the tactics of littoral warfare that include expeditionary operations. Duels between single combatants were common in the era of fighting sail and under engine power in the Civil War. The intricate battle between the

USS *Constitution* and HMS *Guerrier* is a famous example. I have included a short, sweet, and only slightly less famous vignette describing how Lieutenant William B. Cushing sank CSS *Albemarle* in the Civil War—by courage and persistence when outgunned and also when confronted by a series of Confederate defenses. Duels, whether between ships, aircraft, or submarines, had distinctive tactics because there was no need for units in a formation to cooperate.

Vignettes by James Stavridis, Theodore Gatchel, Thomas Cutler, and Thomas and Trent Hone illustrate the greater domain of "handling forces in battle." Although the anthology does not include nuclear war, I will even assert that had a nuclear exchange occurred between the United States and the Soviet Union, the "handling of 'strategic' weapons in battle" (see my book *Fleet Tactics and Coastal Combat*) would have been tactics executed on an intercontinental scale! Without doubt, today's intermediate-range missiles with conventional warheads entail new offensive and defensive tactics, as I point out in the final vignette, "Missile Chess: A Parable."

The physical domain of naval operations has changed and with it the nature of tactics. Through most of history littoral warfare was carried out in a narrow strip of interactions along a coast, but it now will extend several hundred miles to seaward and into the land. Today the air-land-sea interface of littoral combat must be interpreted as a battle from and to the sea in which warships participate. It has become important to understand the distinctly different challenges of littoral waters and the open ocean. This Wheel Book will distinguish them, but it will also elucidate the common tactical characteristics of both.

A truth common to all tactics is that the only way to make no mistakes is to make no decisions. In the battle to retake the Falkland Islands, Rear Admiral John "Sandy" Woodward, who was the theater and tactical commander, was remarkably farsighted in deploying and employing his forces, but that did not prevent losses inflicted by skilled and courageous Argentine pilots. Combat is not in the domain of perfection; it is about being good enough to win a battle. Casualty-free battles are seldom in the nature of combat. Nevertheless, I include one example of perfect execution from the missile age. Abraham Rabinovich describes herein how little Israeli Saar boats won several battles without losing a ship.

Another truth about all tactics is that decisions are made with incomplete information. A successful tactician knows that to win he must be better informed than the enemy. But combat is a two-sided process, and if one waits until he has a complete picture he is likely to suffer a successful enemy attack. I do not approve of naval historians who seek out flaws in the losers' battle plans and tactics. The way to profit from history is to put oneself in the shoes of the tactical decision maker as he confronts a many-faceted problem in an atmosphere of uncertainty. In this way we see what the commander saw and have a better understanding of why he did what he did. John Lundstrom's account of the Battle of Midway is superb from beginning to end, because he describes a victory from brilliant judgment calls in the midst of uncertainties. I have decided the best concise way to illustrate American decisions and moral courage at Midway is to include part of a chapter in which Lundstrom foreshadows the battle and our preparations for it.

A third common property is that battles at sea are infrequent, and so victories are often determined by peacetime preparations to be as ready as possible after a long absence of fighting. In the age of the big gun, roughly 1890 to 1930, there were only seven decisive, war-winning battles as Alfred Thayer Mahan promoted them. Giuseppe Fioravanzo describes several. I have chosen his description of the Battle of the Yalu in the Sino-Japanese War of 1894, passing over Jutland because it was inconclusive tactically though decisive strategically. The chapters by James Rentfrow and Bradley Fiske covering American tactical development before World War I are included because they are instructive for today's U.S. Navy, which has not fought a fleet action for a very long time. The countervailing pressures to keep "steaming as before" in the peacetime environment were frustrating for forward-looking officers like Stephen B. Luce and Fiske himself, when fleet composition and tactical proficiency could not be tested in wartime.

This little volume is an attempt to indicate the breadth of modern combat as a two-sided coin, tactics on one side and technology on the other. Frank Andrews illustrates the challenges in the 1960s of adapting tactics to the new technologies of air and submarine warfare when the U.S. Navy was focused on the growing capabilities of the Soviet navy.

The reader will note that some of the works include biographical information about the individual authors and others do not. This is because of the age of some of the works and because of differing practices over the many years that these works span. Whenever possible, biographical information has been included.

A Wheel Book of the best advice is a personal thing. The handbooks I kept had my ships' characteristics, a record of ship handling evolutions, and the fleet's current composition. I was fortunate to be commissioned in 1952 when the quite explicit Fleet Tactical Publications of World War II were still robust enough to serve as the basis for tactics to fight the Soviet Union. But that changed during my years at sea. This anthology serves as a reminder that in times of geopolitical flux, a fleet's new purposes must foster changes in its composition, and battle tactics must change as well.

An argument has raged over the centuries about whether tactics are an art or a science. With many caveats, the following is a personal opinion about the art and science of warfare.

—Policy and strategy that determine national ends are almost pure *art*, being dominated by subtlety and subjectivity to which scientific and quantitative methods cannot add much.

—Tactics, serving as the means to achieve the ends, are a *blend* of both science and art. The value of science is illustrated by operations analysis and quantitative calculations, while the role of art is illustrated by the unique insights of great leaders who could reduce complex considerations into clear and executable battle plans.

—Between strategy and tactics is campaign planning, which the U.S. Navy has recently labeled "operational art" to conform to Joint Publications. But a naval campaign is mostly about logistics: the delivery and sustainment of forces in a theater of operations. Thus operational art is dominated by the *science* of moving ships, fuel, ammunition, stocks, and troops effectively and efficiently—and when necessary, repairing or replacing them.

For the sake of compactness I have, reluctantly, omitted most end-/footnotes. Additionally, because citations are here included as they appeared in the original selection, they may be of less utility than in the original document. I hope to inspire readers to enrich their knowledge of naval tactics by seeking out the original works, citations and all.

1 "ANCHORAGE"

(Selection from chapter 12 of *Fleet Tactics and Coastal Combat*)

CAPT Wayne P. Hughes Jr., USN (Ret.)

At the beginning of Chapter 1, both the first (1986) and second (1999) editions of *Fleet Tactics* begin with a narrative of the Battle of the Nile in 1798, to illustrate abiding "cornerstones" of all fleet tactics throughout all history:

- Men Matter Most
- Doctrine is the Glue of Tactics
- To Know Tactics, Know Technology
- The Seat of Purpose is on the Land
- Attack Effectively First

In the battle, the commander of the French forces, Vice Admiral François-Paul Brueys d'Aiguilliers, is surprised by Rear Admiral Horatio Nelson, even though both fleets are in sight of each other. The result is the utter destruction of the French fleet by the Royal Navy. The first edition, *Fleet Tactics: Theory and Practice*, then concludes with an imaginary "Second Battle of the Nile" on the two-hundredth anniversary of the first one. This time a Soviet fleet in the Eastern Mediterranean is destroyed by an American tactical commander. But in 1998 the Soviet commander is defeated by a surprise attack from an undetected enemy. In 1798 the British fleet won with lethal gunfire from ships of the line firing from point-blank range. In 1998 the American fleet wins with salvoes of lethal Harpoon missiles launched by American missile ships of an imaginary "*Cushing* class" that conduct their sneak attack from over the horizon. In the two hundred years between the first and second battles of the Nile, fighting fleets went through four stages of tactical and material development, from the era of fighting sail, to the era of armored battleships, to the era of the aircraft carrier, to the era of missile ships and aircraft.

Happily the Soviet Union collapsed before the Second Battle of the Nile could be fought in 1998. Therefore, the second edition of *Fleet Tactics and Coastal Combat* needed a new imaginary battle to illustrate modern fleet tactics. I called it the Battle of the Aegean, and I offer it to illustrate contemporary fleet tactics as the first chapter of this anthology. In composing it I had the fun of keeping the same American commander, but who is now promoted to theater commander. My *Cushings* are also back to play a crucial role in the battle once again.

Written fifteen years ago, the Battle of the Aegean is perhaps even more relevant today, to illustrate what might happen in a maritime conflict with China, for constraining Iranian ambitions, or for helping our allies in Europe and East Asia deter a resurgent Russia. The battle does not look like anything in the American experience or anything the U.S. Navy is trained to fight. To begin with, it demonstrates the difficulty of distinguishing a twenty-first-century battle from a campaign that will inevitably involve widely distributed, cooperating forces. As you read the Battle of the Aegean, look for these important characteristics:

—Modern battles at sea and near a shore are now spread out in such a way that each geographically separated fleet component can play a complementary role.

—Only surface warships are able to maintain control of the sea surface, but a problem is created when one of them is put out of action. Valuable warships must be protected and saved at great effort.

—Submarines exploit their invisibility with a unique capacity for surprise attack. But there are shallow and coastal waters where high-performance nuclear submarines (SSNs) should be risked only as a last resort.

—Carrier aviation is constrained because the purpose of the Battle of the Aegean is not the pursuit of victory against an enemy homeland but the opposite: to prevent a big war from spilling over onto the land.

—Similarly, there are limits on expeditionary force employment. An amphibious commander's first aim must be to keep his forces safe and be ready to insert ground forces ashore where necessary.

—For inshore fighting there is no substitute for small combatants that can be risked in waters cluttered with islands, fishing boats, and coastal traffic.

"ANCHORAGE"

(Selection from chapter 12 of *Fleet Tactics and Coastal Combat*) by CAPT Wayne P. Hughes Jr., USN (Ret.) (Naval Institute Press, 1999): 318–47.

Fiction and Forecasts

Wargaming has a long and honorable history. In the United States "seminar" games with role-playing in possible campaigns is a popular form to assess the strategies of the contending parties, often with participation by other states and organizations such as the UN, NATO, ASEAN, and the European Union. Strategic games are thought-experiments. They explore circumstances similar to those in the Balkans or the Middle East which could escape containment. They are most useful when the military assessments have been treated and the players have, or believe they have, a fair understanding of the military aspects, should the situation degenerate into warfare as an extension of politics.

Other games are intended for military assessments. One series of games was conducted between the world wars at the Naval War College. In that twenty-two-year period, 318 games were played on the maps and game floor in Luce Hall at Newport, Rhode Island.[1] The games were the opposite of the thought-experiments described above. At Newport the strategic setting was settled or assumed. The games were played in detail to test the military consequences of the postulated circumstances. Several of them pitted the U.S. Navy against the Royal Navy, but not because a war with Great Britain was regarded as likely, much less desirable. A test against the Royal Navy was regarded as the supreme challenge to American naval capability, mobility, tactics, and organization.

For substantive strategic study and campaign planning, Japan was the significant opponent. This was so even in the 1920s before friction arose between the Japanese and American governments in the following decade. Of the 137 campaign or strategic games, 127 were played against "Orange," or Japan. The evolution and usefulness of these games in the development of the U.S. Navy's Pacific Ocean campaign plan has been concisely described by Michael Vlahos in his 1986 *Naval War College Review* article. Because operations analysis as we know it today did not yet exist, tactical games were the analytical tool of choice for exploring new tactics and technologies. These included the size, configuration, and employment of aircraft carriers, the preferable types and mix of scouting aircraft, and operations that employed such aircraft in search plans. Vlahos records 106 purely tactical games, of which 71 were fleet actions.

Books of fiction by single authors forecasting future wars and their consequences have a more checkered history. Some have been blatant propaganda. A superb example was Erskine Childers' popular *The Riddle of the Sands*. First published in England in 1903, it was republished by the Naval Institute Press in 1991 and also made into a movie. Childers creates the story of two Englishmen on holiday who sail their yacht among the islands and tidewaters off the German coast. They discover a fleet of barges moored in Imperial Germany's coastal estuaries and an impending invasion of England. The danger of a surprise landing on the English coast to overcome the feeble British army was an obsession felt deeply by Childers. His novel was vivid enough to draw the attention of the press, the public, and Whitehall, as was his purpose. *The Riddle of the Sands* lives on in Oxford and Cambridge student culture as mythology more attuned to their modern ears than *Beowulf* or *The Iliad*. It is the best of its time. But, as Eric Grove writes in his introduction to the 1991 edition, "His book was far from being the only exercise in literary scaremongering at the time." Grove lists half a dozen others, such as *The Great War in England in 1897* by William Le Queux.

A novel similar in stature to Childers' work but written as entertainment is Tom Clancy's *Red Storm Rising*. Produced before the collapse of the Soviet Union, it describes the "real" war between NATO and the Warsaw Pact, and includes some campaign moves and countermoves by the opposing sides that broke the bounds of conventional Pentagon gaming and analysis. By 1986, when the book was published, planning had become somewhat sterile and stereotyped. Clancy's imaginative ideas were treated with respect and examined closely. These works of fiction involve the thoughts and actions of the imagined participants in vivid detail. Unlike the body of science fiction tracing from H. G. Wells' *The War of the Worlds*, some of them are immediate enough to be taken seriously.

Standing apart from fiction are what may be called forecasts. These can be short or long, but they omit the conversations and streams of consciousness of the *dramatis personae*. The best is Hector C. Bywater's *The Great Pacific War: A History of the American-Japanese Campaign of 1931–1933*. Bywater was a journalist and military commentator. Writing in 1925, he describes the imagined events of a short, sharp conflict between the United States and Japan from the point of view of a well-informed and insightful observer. Bywater's stated purpose was to caution Japan against arousing the sleepy American giant, which in the mid-1920s had hardly begun to modernize the fleet left over after the Washington Disarmament Treaty of 1921.

The power of Bywater's argument rested entirely on the acuity of his story. It is only a slight exaggeration to say that in one book, written fifteen years before the real thing, Bywater assembled most of the lessons it took Naval War College gamers twenty years to deduce. He predicts a Japanese surprise attack before the declaration of war—on the Panama Canal. Closing the canal eliminates the entire Atlantic Fleet for the first two months of hostilities. He foresees Japan's swift invasion of the Philippines in a landing at Lingayen Gulf, simultaneous with the seizure of Guam. The U.S. Asiatic Fleet is crushed in the process, while the Pacific Fleet, with neither cruising radius nor logistic ships, must fume in frustration.

And the war proceeds, as Marine and army units and transports to carry them are built up at Pearl Harbor concurrent with distracting Japanese attacks in the Aleutians and along the Oregon-California coast. Both sides attempt ambushes and both suffer from lack of scouting. Already search aircraft are a precious resource in short supply. In a temporizing move reminiscent of Guadalcanal operations, the U.S. Navy blocks a Japanese thrust to take American Samoa. The Japanese invade China and are getting bogged down in its vastness. The American fleet, now built up, begins its majestic sweep through the Central Pacific, seizing Truk, which is not, in Bywater's war, the bastion it will become by 1944. The climactic fleet action is in the vicinity of Yap, a sort of 1932 compression of two great naval battles in 1944, off the Marianas in June and around Leyte Gulf in October. The Japanese of 1932, not faced with President Roosevelt's proclaimed policy of unconditional surrender, immediately thereafter sue for a negotiated but humbling peace. . . .

Epilogue: The Battle of the Aegean

The subject of this edition extends to the operational level and campaigns in littoral waters. It is fitting to replace the tactical example with a scenario expanded to include a typically intricate campaign setting within which a commander must operate to achieve his tactical goal. I indulge in author's license to allow the tactical commander of the first edition to reappear, this time as the operational commander. I need him again, for his skills are going to be tested to the limit. Intended to illustrate tactical simplicity amid operational intricacy, my fable is fiction in that it is seen through a commander's eyes in order to flavor the problem with the human aspects of what we analysts sometimes reduce to mere cold calculation. It is forecast in its description of the modern tactical environment, dominated by sensors, missiles, and information operations, with undercurrents of torpedoes, mines, and amphibious operations.

I confront my Navy hero with the kind of operational problem and tactical situation that the U.S. Navy will face when it is opposed by a respectable, integrated coastal defense, partly ship- and partly land-based. To create such an enemy I have risked offending a friend of the United States and the American navy. I would wish that my "opponent" sees the scenario as constructed for the same purpose that the U.S. Navy played its war games against the British navy in the 1920s. He is chosen not because he is a likely foe but because his seaward-looking forces are a formidable test of the American navy's tactics, systems, and doctrine.

On the other hand, I am quite serious about one aspect of the scenario not found in contemporary U.S. military planning. That is the possibility of a *maritime* campaign in which all the fighting is confined to the seaward side of a coastline. The campaign is one in which any attempt to bring the whole weight of American military power to bear against the enemy homeland would be disastrously contrary to American interests. At the same time to allow the foe the unimpeded use of his home waters would be just as intolerable. The U.S. Navy must carry a maritime campaign all the way to the enemy coast because the United States is a maritime nation.

The narrative shows the extent to which warfare in coastal waters requires tactics, doctrine, and combat systems substantially different from those of the American blue-water navy. By a combat system I mean ships, aircraft, and sensors all connected for unified action by information technology and combat doctrine. The successful interweaving is to my mind the essence and intent of network-centric warfare. At the same time the vignette is intended to show why an opponent who is fighting in his own waters does not need the same high technology to defend himself that we will need to penetrate his coastal defenses. Doctrine for semiautonomous operations combined with concealment and surprise will be sufficient for an enemy to challenge us to the utmost. Indeed, the circumstances facing my hero, Admiral Grant, are so severe that I have had to give him some forces not now in the American navy, for I do not think Grant can meet his challenge without them.

Beyond those things, I do not intend the tactics as lessons learned, except to illustrate that in combat the devil is in the details of the weapons, sensors, and doctrine employed. For instance, an influential feature of the scenario will be that all three countries involved have large numbers of Harpoon missiles. Another fundamental characteristic is a variety of combatants small enough to risk in combat, using networking to concentrate fire in time and space. Nuclear powered submarines are of little value at the climax, but they loom large at the onset of the crisis by playing their traditional role. Neither land- nor sea-based aircraft strikes contribute to the solution itself, but a perceptive reader will see that aircraft on *both* sides everywhere cast a long shadow over every tactical action.

The Crisis

Before him lies living proof, thinks Adm. Ulysses S. "Sam" Grant, that operations are more intricate than tactics. His battle plan depends on reducing all considerations to a set of simple tactical actions that everyone understands well enough to carry out in the midst of the confusion and uncertainty of the impending fight. But the operations now under way flow from layer on layer of national policy and military strategy. There will be a battle because of a sequence of deadly events that had not been pretty for the U.S. Navy. Sam Grant would give the battle his full and undivided attention soon, but first he goes over in his mind the multifaceted decisions that initiated the campaign now rushing to its climax.

The setting embraces not two but three antagonists, as well as vested interests of every country in Europe and most in western Asia. There have been more Byzantine circumstances than those surrounding him, thinks Grant, but his are sufficiently convoluted to make it fitting that ancient Byzantium is no farther from him now than the far side of the Aegean Sea. His mission is to cool the passions of the two ancient antagonists on each side of it.

Sam Grant's operational responsibility is to interpose between Turkey and Greece at this, the eleventh hour before all the dogs of war are unleashed. The United States' peacemaking endeavor is down to its last chance, a chance that rests on a battle by his forces alone. It is the American admiral's paradox that in order to restore peace he must shed blood. A battle is certain but the outcome is not, because the U.S. Sixth Fleet, unaided, faces the entire Turkish navy and more. Yet his battle plan can be successful because the mission is attainable by the tacticians under his command. With luck and skill and staunchness his forces will be just sufficient to the task. It is going to be the American navy's greatest challenge since the Battle of Midway.

How Admiral Grant came to wear the mantle of a combat commander is itself one of those marvels of strategic intricacy. U. S. Grant is CINCUS-NAVEUR, who until just three days ago was subordinate to the American theater commander in Europe, USCINCEUR, the formidable four-star General E. F. "Famous" Grouse, up north in land-locked Stuttgart, Germany. Grouse was no friend of Grant's; in his mind all military decisions worthy of the name resulted from action on the ground. Yet after the opening violence, Grant found himself in command and taking orders directly from the secretary of defense and chairman of the JCS. The president, in his delicate calibration of the politics of violence, is committed to succeed or fail with the Navy alone. Using the modest forces of the Sixth Fleet and without the full weight of American might, Grant must bank the fires of the simmering feud between Turkey and Greece, so much in its passions like the ageless hatred between the Capulets and Montagues—or in American imagery, the Hatfields and McCoys.

In recent months Greek zealots fomented violence on Cyprus that was beyond containment by the small UN peacekeeping force. A week ago Greece used the violence as the reason to announce its intentions to introduce theater ballistic missiles into the island, missiles that in a matter of minutes could reach every vital center in Turkey. The Turkish populace was enraged. Uncharacteristically, the president and prime minister of Turkey both supported the popular anger and nurtured the swelling demand for action. As it came down to Grouse and Grant from the CIA through the Joint Staff, Turkish forces were about to effect a strategy they had prepared should Greece ever act on its threat to move missiles into Cyprus.

Publicly Turkey's minister of defense announced a quarantine to block the Greek movement to Cyprus by sea. Simultaneously, Turkey prepared to sail in force against Cyprus so ostentatiously that no official in Greece could fail to respond. For Turkey had a deeper motive. Far to the east of Greece and tucked less than 100 miles away from the Turkish mainland, Cyprus was bait in a trap. The Greek navy, supportable only weakly by the Greek air force, which must fly to the end of its tether, would have to run a deadly gauntlet. Turkish aircraft, surface warships, submarines, and land-launched missiles were poised to fight a littoral war that was vastly in Turkey's favor. As the climax and conclusion of phase one in Turkey's campaign plan, a fleet action was planned west of Cyprus which would reduce the Greek navy to impotence and lead to phase two, which would be centered in the Aegean Sea.

Greek Intentions and Turkish Response

① Greece Plans to move land-launched TBMs to Cyprus
② Turkey announces intention to move major forces into Cyprus, and then
③ Crush the Greek navy

In the Aegean lay the true object of Turkish ambitions. Over many years Greece and Turkey had shaped their naval forces and tactics to confront each other. In Aegean waters the outcome of a fleet encounter was thought by both to be a toss-up, with perhaps the nod to Greece. Greeks owned (in their eyes) or occupied (as seen in Turkey) the many islands of the Dodecanese and Cyclades and expected to use them to ambush Turkish ships and aircraft in those confined waters with missiles and armed aircraft. But if Turkey destroyed the Greek navy first, then the islands could be isolated and all doors opened into the Aegean.

It had become intolerable for Turkey that with sovereignty over those islands Greece now dominated the Aegean. It was bad enough to suffer at the whim of a Greek government whose islands and navy could de facto close its vital sea lane through the Aegean into the Dardanelles and Black Sea. Then in 1995 Greece had extended its territorial waters to twelve miles in accordance with the UN's Convention on the Law of the Sea of November 1994. If Greece ever enforced the terms of the UN treaty—and it had never denied itself the right to do so—by international law it would de jure control access to the Black Sea and every port on Turkey's west coast.

Beyond that, the Greek Islands influenced—in some eyes determined—the demarcation of the continental shelf for the purpose of establishing underwater mineral rights. Attempts at oil exploration under Turkish auspices had led to protests of encroachment from Greece. Authority over airspace and air traffic in the Aegean and militarization of the Greek islands near the Turkish coast were other grievances still unresolved. From these many aggravations, the littoral waters off the west coast of Turkey took on the color of two armed camps. The final straw came when Turkish intelligence learned that Greece had surreptitiously introduced cruise missiles into Cos, Lemnos, and Chios. From that moment the armed forces of Turkey commenced to lay the plans now in motion to seize the islands and their missiles, as well as Samos and Lesbos. After that the government would strike the best bargain it could achieve in the courts of public opinion, striving for justice and a better balance in the Aegean.

Turkish Strategy, Phase 2

Amphibious operations against Limnos, Lesbos, Chios, Samos, and Cos from Ayvalik, Cesme, Izmir, Kusadasi, and Bodrum

It mattered not a whit whether the Greek navy understood the Turks' two-pronged strategy to fight first at Cyprus and then in the eastern Aegean, for no Greek government could survive if Cyprus was abandoned. The Greek navy would have to risk all in one throw of dice that would be loaded in Turkey's favor. NATO was appalled, for Turkey and Greece were both members. The crisis that the other NATO nations had sought to avoid for over fifty years was upon them and they were helplessly divided. The United Nations was caught in irons too, split as they were between friendships on both sides of the Aegean. If there was to be an enforced peace it would be by American action.

American Policy Decisions

When he learned the Turkish strategy, President Rainsford C. G. Harris, Princeton graduate and fervent admirer of Greek and Western civilization, was ready to intervene on the merits of the case: Turkey was the aggressor; Turkey must be stopped. At the same time Harris must persuade Greece, for its own good and the naval balance in the Aegean, to defer to U.S. diplomacy backed by the force of the Sixth Fleet. The State Department was more level-headed: democratic Turkey was a wedge of civilization reaching into the Asian continent. It was a country that understood and spoke the ethos of Islam while rejecting the zealotry of Moslem theocracies. It was a strong state, struggling for stability, hopeful of prosperity, that had sought and received the friendship of the United States and NATO during the years when it was the easternmost outpost of the West's confrontation with the Soviet Union. Secretary of State Dan M. Tinker's sympathies were with Turkey and its people who, he thought, had for years been more than patient over the many provocations heaped upon them by the Greek Cypriot majority.

The two views coalesced from opposite poles into one American action. In the eyes of the National Security Council this was a maritime crisis for which there should and would be a naval solution. For fifty years the U.S. Navy had interposed off Taiwan, the Levant, Africa, and Central America; in the South China Sea; and in southwest Asia. Though the Navy's effect on the landward side was imperfect, when a maritime issue was at stake, as was the case now in the eastern Mediterranean, the Navy could boast unblemished success since 1949. Nor had any attack been consummated against it except by accident or with that impersonal weapon, the mine.

Hence the NSC proposed to interpose two Aegis cruisers between Cyprus and the ports of Iskenderun and Mersin, where Turkish soldiers would soon embark for a strongly protected move to Cyprus. The American ambassador in Ankara was instructed to carry a coldly correct diplomatic note to Prime Minister Yusuf Bey to the effect that any move toward Cyprus was a move against the United States of America. President Harris would publicly declare the single thing on which he and Secretary Tinker were in accord: neither Greek nor Turkish ships and aircraft would be allowed to fire on the other, or alter the military balance in Cyprus, with missiles, troops, or anything else. To give this weight, Harris would speak by video teleconference to President Hatzopoulos of Greece to assure him that no ships would approach Cyprus until passed upon by the U.S. Navy. Hatzopoulos agreed to stand aside, but not cheerfully, for his own navy's passions were aroused. Meanwhile, in Ankara the interview had not gone well for the American ambassador. He could only report that his diplomatic note suffered curt dismissal by a stolid and stoic prime minister.

The Campaign Begins

Those difficult events had transpired by 26 July, only five days ago. As theater naval commander, Grant's views had been solicited, of course. When he heard the plan from General Grouse, he said COMSIXTHFLT, Vice Admiral Paul T. "Patent" Anchor, would direct Aegis ships to start eastward at once. But Grant asked for and was granted the following additional provisions:

- Four, not two, Aegis warships would interpose off Cyprus in pairs northeast and northwest of the island.
- Three submarines would move into the same waters, unannounced and invisible.
- The carrier battle force, one CVN and four escorts, would be brought to full readiness 150 miles from Turkey, with sufficient sea room for defense in depth but close enough to cover the interposing American warships.

Meanwhile Grant moved the three-ship amphibious ready group well to the west. Afloat, the Marines expeditionary unit should be protected, but all eight of his Aegis ships were committed. He contemplated but discarded the idea of moving the Marines ashore. Therefore he dispatched what was left: eight little 800-ton *Cushings* tied up to a short wharf next to the submarine tender at La Maddalena in Sardinia. Offensive ships, the *Cushings* were not configured for escort, but Grant wanted them under way, free of any Italian interference. They were to rendezvous with the three ships of the ARG and loiter in the Tyrrhenian Sea. *Cushings* are intended for short swift missions and not for sustained steaming. Grant was promised reinforcements from the Atlantic Fleet in ten days. Until then, the eight crews, sixty each, would have to tough it out with the ARG. But the corvettes had drilled for sustained crisis operations before and Grant had confidence that Commander Gridley,[2] the tactical commander, would keep them at the ready.

U.S. Sixth Fleet Interposes

① DDGs *Arleigh Burke* and *John Paul Jones*
② CGs *Ticonderoga* and *Valley Forge*
③ SSNs *Annapolis, Chicago,* and *San Francisco*
④ CVN *Ronald Reagan* with CG *Gettysburg*, DDG *O'Kane*, and DDs *Leftwich* and *Harry W. Hill*
⑤ ARG moving west

1 Turkish troops embarking
2 Supporting airfields

In the amphibious ships is a detachment of SEALs, experts in special warfare, for whom Grant envisioned a possible role. So he has ordered to sea the three operative PCs from their base in Rota, Spain, with instructions to pick up the SEALs from the amphibs north of Sardinia and then head east.

Also at Rota is a 40,000-ton mother ship capable of carrying eight 200-ton Killer-Scouts and ten STOVL aircraft at a speed of thirtytwo knots. Altogether there are thirty of the lethal 200-ton vessels, configured variously for inshore missions and tasks. Twelve of the thirty, called *Phantoms*, are armed with tactical land-attack missiles. Grant ordered the mother ship to load eight *Phantoms* in its well deck and sail eastward into the Mediterranean, with the PCs in company.

The Shocks

As Admiral Grant feared, the Turks were not deterred. On 28 July, just before midnight, the first attack took place during the change of the watch in the USS *Ticonderoga*'s CIC. It came in the form of eighteen land-, air-, and sea-launched, American-made Harpoon missiles that approached from all points of the compass. The *Tico* and her consort, the *Valley Forge*, dealt with seventeen of them, but one of the ASCMs penetrated and struck the *Tico* amidships, putting her dead in the water and out of action. The *Valley Forge*, distracted while rendering assistance, was then struck in the next attack at 0025 on the twenty-ninth by one penetrating Harpoon, knocking out her missile battery. While the other two Aegis ships rushed to assist from sixty miles away, eight more Turkish Harpoons arrived. Five missed or were defeated by soft-kill, but two struck one ship and one the other, rendering both derelict. At 0230 the two undamaged DDGs arrived, circled, and sweated until fleet tugs could arrive from Naples. The attacks stopped. Turkey either had no other Harpoons at the ready, was husbanding those remaining, or felt that the destruction was enough. In the two crippled warships there were ninety casualties.

Immediately after that, the Turks, thinking the way was clear, sailed an army brigade in five LSTs and two transports heavily escorted with destroyers and frigates, all under intense air cover. But the three U.S. SSNs were lurking nearby. One detected, trailed, and called in a second. The two penetrated the screen in tandem and at 0410 sank an LST and both transports in six minutes. Seven hundred Turkish soldiers and sailors perished.

After assimilating the facts of the disaster, at 0530 on 29 July General Grouse spoke personally to the chairman of the JCS, in the middle of the night in Washington. He demanded the removal of Admiral Grant and proposed to bring down the full weight of American firepower on Turkey with massive air and missile strikes. Further, he said, he had put U.S. Army forces on full alert. Grouse subscribed to JCS doctrine of full spectrum dominance through comprehensive situational awareness and precision strike. But the chairman reflected on the prudent measures Grant had taken and the fact that Grant was his best fighting admiral. He and the secretary of defense were as appalled at Grouse's heedless adherence to doctrine as they were at Turkey's deep-seated determination and the bloodshed of the stunning attacks. Five hours later, at 0600 Washington time, they met with the president and within the hour received his endorsement, first, to order Grouse to keep his planes on the ground and troops in their barracks. Second, they concluded that if there was to be any hope of the United States forestalling the outbreak of war, then the conflict must be confined to the sea. The chairman believed that this was feasible because it would be what Turkey wanted as well. Turkey had somehow to be stopped from moving into the Aegean, yet without hitting Turkish territory. Since the American role was to be strictly maritime, a skip-echelon command structure designated Admiral Grant the ad hoc combatant commander.

Concurrently the president and secretary of state had to move heaven and earth to bring the Turkish government to its senses. World opinion must be brought to bear, while Greece was kept on the sidelines with assurances that no Aegean island would fall to Turkey. A somewhat chastened president now agreed that Turkey could be told, through the Russians perhaps, that the world would look sympathetically on its frustrations once it abandoned its intention of forcible entry into the Greek islands.

Even before the NSC meeting, the commander-in-chief set the wheels in motion. Still in disagreement, Grouse resigned. At 1400 Naples time on 29 July, Grant was told his mission was to keep Turkish forces from seizing the Greek islands and without touching Turkish soil! In the fifteen minutes it takes the secretary of defense and chairman to outline the situation as seen from Washington, Grant has formulated a solution to his knotty problem. He asks, does "soil" exclude the Turkish transports in port? The secretary mumbles and the chairman blinks. Grant concludes that he has all the official sanction he is going to get. They will have the details of his plan soon enough.

At once Grant summons his staff, outlines his concept, and asks for a swift estimate of the situation. The staff see a major alternative to the Turkish investment of the islands by sea to be airborne invasion. For various reasons Grant concludes that if the Turks do not believe they control the coastal waters to move safely by ship then they will not attack at all.[3]

That settled, next the staff makes the calculations for an operation order and rapidly feed it into a dynamic, geographical plot depicting a host of interlocking movements. By 1900 on the twenty-ninth these have been tweaked and approved by Grant and disseminated electronically to all NAVEUR ships and stations. The Joint Chiefs receive and quickly digest it. For information and in case the conflict escalates, USCINCEUR (acting) also has it.

Enemy Moves

By 2000 on the evening of the same day the Turkish high command accelerates its time table by issuing orders to move troops to the LSTs, LCTs, LCMs, and transports for the short run to the five Greek islands. Simultaneously the Turkish surface fleet is ordered to close on the five ports of embarkation, in order to screen the movement and support the landings. Air Force aircraft are shifted to western Turkey and search and covering tasks assigned. Six modern diesel submarines move into screen stations, and minecraft (unable to match the pace) prepare to lay minefields.

At first light on the thirtieth evidence of Turkish troop, ship, and aircraft redeployments is observed by American satellites. By midmorning clues to the imminent invasion are inserted in global command and control systems displays and text. In Naples via GCCS Grant has the same information held in Washington. Nine destroyers and fast-attack craft will be coming down from the

Dardanelles. He estimates that some of these ships carry Harpoons but most will have shorter range Penguin missiles well suited for the cluttered waters of the northern Aegean. Though he cannot see them on the plot, the entire Ionian coast is blanketed with small patrol boats and fishing vessels employed to supplement Turkish air reconnaissance.

Moving west from the vicinity of Cyprus will be ten Turkish warships clearly identified by satellite as Harpoon shooters. About twenty more Turkish destroyers, frigates, and fast-attack craft are in the naval base at Aksaz on the southwest Anatolian coast. Grant expects all that are able to get under way to join the Cyprus contingent. Thus, he expects to face coming up from the south an enemy force of twenty-five or more destroyers and fast-attack craft, carrying among them about 180 Harpoon missiles. They will enter the Aegean on the evening of 31 July.

Even more crucial to his plan, the satellites have pinpointed the exact locations of the transports and larger amphibious ships in five ports of embarkation: Ayvalik off Lesbos, Cesme and Izmir near Chios, Kusadasi near Samos, and Bodrum adjacent to Cos. The troopship positions are known exactly and the precise latitude and longitude of individual targets have been passed to his ships so that the coordinates can be plugged into their missile guidance systems.

Which missiles? They must be the small ballistic missiles carried in the *Phantoms*. These are normally used for tactical support of Marines or soldiers fighting ashore. Harpoons and Tomahawks are next to useless, for one thing because most of the ports are deeply embedded in the Turkish coast behind terrain that is tricky for cruise missiles to traverse. For another, Turkey will be expecting cruise missiles and has the port defenses to take out most of them. On the other hand, the *Phantoms'* tactical ballistic missiles (TBMs) are so new that Turkey has no defense against them worthy of the name. A navy modification of the army's tactical weapon, they can be delivered with the greatest precision and with a time of flight of only a few minutes. From the outset, Grant had dismissed an air strike from the Sixth Fleet carrier USS *Ronald Reagan*, in part because there would be too much collateral damage to the port cities, in part because over two hundred Turkish fighters would be arrayed against them. The

Sixth Fleet's four submarines must stay in a blocking position between Turkey and Cyprus. They cannot cover all the ports in the Aegean, nor does he want SSNs tangling with Turkish mines and diesel submarines in the Ionian coast's shallow waters.

The Tactical Plan

To deliver their TBMs the *Phantoms* must not just survive to reach their launch positions within ninety miles of the targeted ports. They must do so before the Turkish transports and LSTs get under way. Movement, even slow movement, is the friend of surface ships and foe of long-range missiles, especially in the cluttered coastal environment. Furthermore, Grant's information is not firm as to where the Turks are headed. They have much better knowledge than he of the beaches and Greek defenses. Once the transports are under way his problem is unsolvable. That is what he saw instantly when his mission was briefed to him by the chairman, and why he needed passive acquiescence to hit the transports in their ports where their locations were known to within a few meters.

Grant long ago had concluded that without the new *Phantoms* he had no maritime solution. Eight of them, each with ten small TBMs, will be enough to neutralize nineteen transports and LSTs, ignoring the small landing craft that are too numerous to strike. He estimates that if he takes out half or more of the nineteen large ships, then the Turks cannot proceed and will have to delay long enough for the arrival of the full Atlantic Fleet.

Lieutenant Commander Genda, the tactical commander of the *Phantoms* embarked in his tiny flagship, the *Ninja*, will target all nineteen.[4] Even though there might be a few undiscovered troop ships, Genda's orders are to shoot the works: launch all eighty TBMs in one sudden pulse at the targets located by satellite.

Though eighty missiles against nineteen undefendable targets seem to be ample overkill, Grant does not expect 100 percent coverage. The missiles have bomblets that blanket an area of two football fields that is normally filled with enemy tanks. They are less than ideal ship-killers, but they will wreak havoc to the topsides, electronics, bridges, and probably one deck down in each transport.

If troops are aboard the carnage will be dreadful. Grant hopes to launch his strike before they embark. Of course the loss of life would seal the delay he seeks, but the bloody result of such an attack is hardly the way to soothe Turkish passion or evoke sympathy among the press and world opinion.

The problem is moot. The attack is scheduled for the earliest possible moment. The *Phantoms'* fast carrier is slated to pass south of the Peloponnesus at 1700 on the 31st, an hour behind the *Cushings*. Since the passage will be in daylight and the weather clear, it could be spotted, but Grant thinks that until the *Phantoms* are launched no Turkish alarm bells will ring. The *Phantoms* will enter the water after dark, around 2100, just west of the Cyclades. It will take a courageous Turkish reconnaissance effort to reach across the Greek-dominated waters and a lot of Turkish faith in Greek restraint. From the *Ronald Reagan* an air screen will be flying between the Cyclades and Dodecanese until dark as a false indicator of American intentions.

The big hazard to the *Phantoms* is not the Turks but the Greeks. Will the word from Athens be disseminated? Will the Greeks eschew their own reconnaissance effort? Will scores of Greek ships and aircraft and missile batteries let unidentified ships pass unreported and unmolested? Grant did not reveal his plan to Athens; a leak was too likely. He can afford to lose some aircraft; he will surely lose *Cushings*; he cannot afford to lose *Phantoms*.

After dark the *Phantoms* will glide through the Cyclades. Having no electromagnetic signature, they can only be detected by human eye. Low in the water, small at 200 tons, and stubby so as to fit in their mothership-carrier, even in daylight they are never easy to detect. At night, in a state three sea under a waning moon that will not rise until 0100, there is a good chance that they can penetrate the Cyclades unnoticed by both Greeks and Turks. A chance fisherman or coastal trader will likely see dark shapes with no lights, but a report of their mysterious presence will take time. And no Greek or Turkish missile seeker head can detect and home on a *Phantom*; gunfire and cutlasses are the only weapons against them. They will report their movements and locations to each other covertly via satellite. It bemuses Genda to know his vessels will be almost side by side but virtually invisible to each other. There will be no formation and no mutual support. Any one of them that is picked off must be abandoned, its crew of twelve left on its own.

Genda will take the *Ninja*, *Phantom*, *Ghost*, and *Furtif* northeast and, after clearing the islands, run the last fifty-five miles across open water, though to suppress their wakes the passage will be more like a tiptoe than a sprint.[5] The four will take station just east of the little island of Psara and huddle almost against its coast. There they will rendezvous and await Grant's signal to launch, at 0400 on 1 August. Their targets are in Ayvalik, Cesme, and Izmir.

The second set of four *Phantoms* are under the senior CO, Lieutenant Stephanie Decatur embarked in the *Black Knight*. With the *Sting*, *Mist*, and *Silencioso* she will take a more southerly route, passing slowly, quietly, and separately through the Greek islands, gathering again at their launch point in the shadows of Dhenova north of Amorgos.[6] Their targets are in Cesme, in duplication of the northern task element, and in the ports of Kusadasi and Bodrum alone.

Everything else in the Sixth Fleet is in support of the intended 0400 attack, but the *Cushings* play the indispensable role. Their task, though simple to signal and straightforward, is tactically demanding, hazardous in the extreme, and one for which no other U.S. Navy warship is suited. The eight *Cushings*' task is to draw attention and, no doubt, missile fire from up to twenty-five Turkish warships.

They Are Expendable

Grant had ordered the eight old *Cushings* from their base at La Maddelena to screen the three amphibious ships. Once he saw there would be fighting in the Aegean, he ordered them east. There are seven of them now, because one corvette broke down. They must be at the entrance to the Aegean between Crete and Kithra an hour ahead of the *Phantoms*' mother ship, so he ordered them to arrive there at 1600 on 31 July. They have 500 miles to travel, but because of Grant's foresight they have ample time. He sent them through the Strait of Messina to shorten the distance and also to *increase* the chance that the Turkish navy would know they were coming. For the *Cushings* are his bait; some and perhaps all seven will sacrifice themselves to draw attention from the *Phantoms*.

Years ago twelve *Cushings* had been homeported in the Mediterranean at Grant's insistence when he was Commander Sixth Fleet. They had been crucial in defeating the Soviet fleet on 1 August 1998 in the 1986 edition, which did not foresee the collapse of the Soviet Union. Of the ten now remaining, all eight not in upkeep had put to sea, and seven are coming. Of 800 tons with a crew of sixty, the main armament of each consists of eight Harpoon missiles and a seventy six-millimeter gun. They have meager ASW capability, but that is irrelevant. Each carries a Lamps helicopter. They are similar to dozens of the older designs among the world's best coastal navies. Seven will be enough to play their sacrificial role.

Commander "Ready" Gridley, Grant's own choice, has been in tactical command for a year and has the *Cushing* commanding officers bonded as a team in which each knows what to expect from the others. The tactical execution of the operation that will ensue will be Gridley's, but the tactics are an extension of Grant's own, worked out years ago. The *Cushings* are obsolescent for this mission, because there is a big question whether their Harpoons will penetrate the defenses of Turkish warships. The Turks are similarly armed with their own Harpoon variant. Moreover, the Turkish navy has trained assiduously to defend against Harpoon attacks because that is the principal threat in the Greek surface navy. Turkish skill with and against Harpoons is the penalty of American foreign aid, thinks Grant wryly.

Gridley will pass north of Crete and until dark steer slowly along the coast with radars on and radios blaring tactical signals to assure that the Turks and everyone else knows where he is. Carrier aircraft scouting between the Cyclades and Dodecanese will see any Turkish formation and forestall an ambush. The aircraft will also confirm the satellite information of the enemy's composition. At dusk around 1900 he will alter course radically to port, step up speed to 31 knots, and head for the little island of Anafi. At 2100 the *Cushings* will form two very ragged lines abreast of four and three corvettes. Lateral spacing between ships is an imprecise five miles. The two lines will leapfrog alternately, on signal via laser lamps. Each line in turn will sprint ahead at thirty-five knots plus, while the other dawdles at six in an attempt to look like small, innocuous shipping. Near Anafi at around 2300 they will shape a course eastwards toward the best estimated position of the twenty-five Turkish warships.

Grant's Battle Plan

① ② Movement of Phantoms' mother ship
②③Ⓐ , ②③Ⓑ Movement of Phantoms
Ⓐ Ⓑ Ⓒ Ⓓ Movement of Cushings
Ⓧ - Ⓨ - Ⓩ Expected movement of main Turkish fleet

On a rotational basis, two of their Lamps helicopters will fly south to near the coast of Crete, flying high with radars turned on, for a deception within a deception. If the Turks have studied the *Cushing* tactics, they will expect them to be hugging the coast. On another occasion, the helicopters would be crucial scouts, but tonight with confusing contacts all around, Gridley does not expect them to add much information. He does not know whether the Turkish fleet will have helicopters up and scouting at night. Their role is not a crucial factor, because the enemy has operational knowledge of his presence, and it is only the details of his tactics that he wishes to conceal. If a helicopter approaches from the east to investigate his corvettes, their orders are to shoot it down at eight miles. The American night combat air patrol from the carrier is to intimidate anything in the air moving at fifty knots or greater, everywhere but off the north coast of Crete. Gridley only depends on the jets for harassment and perhaps to chase search aircraft away.

Gridley expects the enemy's screen of Harpoon-armed fast-attack craft to be in a scouting line ahead of the destroyers. If any of their radars are on, then his ships, running silent, will detect first, well within missile range. American and Turkish Harpoons can reach seventy nautical miles, but Gridley expects to launch his weapons at a third of that because of the incipient electromagnetic duel over first detection, tracking, and targeting. Harpoons home with great precision, but the *Cushings* will be shooting where neutral traffic and innocent fishermen can be unintended targets. One *Cushing* only will fire a salvo of not more than three Harpoons down the bearings of any intermittently radiating screen ship. The shooter will then attempt to clear laterally away from a predictable return salvo at high speed and use passive antimissile defenses. The other corvettes will slow and wait for another radiating target. The reason for the puny salvo is because Gridley must attempt to survive as long as possible and drain the Turkish ships of as many missiles as he can. If the Turks approach with radars off, then sharp eyes will determine who sees and shoots first and how well, and guns will be as deadly as missiles. With radars off on both sides it will be an ugly melee, and the smaller force—the *Cushings*—will do less damage to each other!

These actions are well-drilled tactics, the major difference being that the seven *Cushings* with fifty-six Harpoons cannot defeat twenty-five skillful Turkish warships carrying 180 similar missiles of their own, and who are practiced at fighting in their home waters. The *Cushings* must, atypically, husband their missiles in the hope of stretching out the battle. Though always wary, Gridley hopes, even expects, first contact to be east of Astipalaia sometime around midnight. He will draw the enemy west among the islands for as long as the surviving corvettes have the means to fight. Each captain knows he must keep the attention of the Turkish force south of Amorgos, where the four southerly *Phantoms* will be heading.

The chief of staff reminds Grant that Gridley is going to have a fuel problem. Grant is abashed; by such oversights are plans destroyed. But Gridley reports that he will arrive with enough fuel to operate wide open for perhaps three hours and his ships will not be at full throttle all the time. The ships that survive need only limp to the nearest Greek island inlet or harbor.

Grant Moves Aboard

Around noon on 30 July, Grant and his battle staff depart CINCUSNAVEUR headquarters in Naples in two tilt-rotor V-22s, leaving instructions to arrange an emergency meeting with the Greek minister of defense in Athens on the 31st. After landing on the Sixth Fleet flagship, he discusses the electronically transmitted battle plan with Vice Admiral Anchor. His old friend Patent tells Sam he wants a bigger role but concedes that if the *Phantoms* fail he will have more than enough to do in dealing with about 200 enemy aircraft. Grant plays best-of-five acey-deucy with the air wing commander, visits the chaplain, eats mid-rat soup and sandwiches with the aviators, showers, and registers a nap in the flag cabin.

At 0700 on the 31st he has the satellite imagery update via GCCS. It confirms the locations and numbers of Turkish warships in motion. At 0900 he takes off in an escorted S-3 for his meeting in Athens, set for 1300. En route the jets pass the V-22s who are also cleared to land in Athens. On arrival, he devotes his thirty minutes with Defense Minister Loucas to emphasize the message already transmitted from Naples: "If you please, do your utmost to tell everyone with a weapon to hold fire until a Turk tries to land on Greek soil. Strange ships may be sighted almost anywhere. They will be American or Turkish. Please leave them be. Everything depends on every Greek soldier and sailor holding fire." In actuality, Grant's plan does not stand or fall on Greek discipline, but if it breaks down he foresees chaos that will confound his own intentions and could open the floodgates of the war that he is trying to prevent.

At 1400 his staff ostentatiously boards the S-3, which takes off under a flight plan filed for the carrier. Minutes later Grant departs unobserved in one V-22, taking only his flag lieutenant (and communicator) and his operations officer. Grant may be the only one in his command who thinks so, but he is firmly convinced that the battle plan now will survive without him. The crucial action will be by the *Cushings*, and so he has arranged a rendezvous with them south of Cape Matapan. At 1500 the hovering V-22 lowers the three NAVEUR officers to the deck of the flagship, USS *Victory*.

Grant's fear is not that Ready Gridley will be timid; just the opposite, for the tactics they had worked out were all designed to attack effectively first and win. This time success depends on husbanding weapons so that enough *Cushing* firepower survives for an hour or more to sow confusion and draw the enemy's attention away from the *Phantoms* until their eighty tactical ballistic missiles are launched and they clear away to westward. Gridley has his orders, but in the flush of first battle, passion and his killer instinct might take over. Weighing the risks, like an old warhorse Grant believes he should be at the point of attack in the *Victory*. In Naples he is superfluous. His chief of staff is the perfect campaign manager to keep Washington informed and fend off the second-guessers, and the staff does not need him to sort out the inevitable problems of broken parts, emergency supply, or a missed rendezvous.

In the *Victory*, Admiral U. S. Grant sits in the familiar squadron commander's station just behind the pilot and copilot seats. Gridley has the copilot's seat normally occupied by the OOD. Lieutenant Commander Ray Bernotti, the captain, sits at the pilot's console, which controls all operational aspects of the flagship.[7] The OOD has a fold-down seat normally occupied by the Boatswain's Mate of the Watch, while the boatswain's mate stands watch on his feet, the old-fashioned way. The CINCUSNAVEUR ops officer and flag lieutenant sit on campstools. It is a bit of a squeeze.

One of the terrible things about this war is that he, Grant, is fighting an old friend. He first met and played squash with the present Commander-in-Chief of Turkish Naval Forces, Mehmet Abdul, in a port visit to Izmir when they were lieutenants. Their families grew close when Mehmet attended the Command and Staff course at the Naval War College fifteen years ago. Later, as staff officers they plotted and schemed how they might coordinate a NATO operation against the Soviets in the Black Sea. The personal side of it is painful, but in addition both friends know how the other thinks about tactics. Mehmet will know Sam had something up his sleeve. There are not many opponents as mentally prepared to combat Grant and the Sixth Fleet as Admiral Abdul.

Sam Grant regrets an oversight: he might have disembarked some of the *Cushings* to save lives, for not all sixty of each crew will be needed to serve the guns this night. He muses over the personal risk. If the plan fails, Grouse will get his wish after all; Grant will be relieved and court-martialed. If it succeeds there will still be raised eyebrows because he did not manage the battle in the conventional way. If he has misjudged the skill of Commander Gridley's captains and crews or underestimated the enemy, then they will all soon be dead. The crews know the odds in a detached way, but they have never been in battle and with the optimism of youth think they are immortal.

Besides, the *Cushings* trust me, Sam Grant, who beat the Soviets and has never lost a battle. This time, if I have assessed the battle correctly, more than half the *Cushings* will be sunk or out of action; and a quarter of these sailors, the best anywhere, will be casualties.

That is the personal side. As combatant commander the important operational question is, will my plan work? If not, it will be because the *Phantoms* have also suffered severely, for there is enough overkill in their firepower that only a strange, unfortuitous event can defeat the attack. The TBMs have been tested, but never in battle. The intelligence is the best in the world, but it could have been deceived in plotting the Turkish ships. Grant's assessment must be right that the troopships will still be pier-side at the time of the TBM attack.

If the *Phantoms* fail, then there will be bloody war. The rest of his Sixth Fleet, at the point of the sword, will be punished. Worse, the prestige of the United States will be in shambles, the Greeks will fight, the weakened Turks will be caught in a disaster of their own making, and the potential chaos in the eastern Mediterranean and southwestern Asia is incalculable.

All will be revealed in six hours, thinks Grant. Yes, the operation will succeed because it is sound. I didn't join this profession for its certainties. The life is sweet if not assured. Truly few things are safe and sure in war, yet the pieces are in place. He has assembled the forces to execute a good plan. The young commanding officers of the *Phantoms* and *Cushings* are well trained in sound doctrine and the ships manned by crews able to stay up with swift and sudden warfare in these confining, confounding coastal waters.

Grant turns to the tactical commander and says, "Your weapons are free, Gridley."

Denouement

In one aspect only can the outcome of Grant's battle plan be reasonably forecast. It is that the *Phantoms* will launch their missiles on time and knock out enough Turkish amphibious capacity to fulfill the mission.

A novelist would be obligated to produce the rest of the story—the battle itself. The author would create an aura of inevitability about the results. If she aspires to contemporary mores, then Grant must have feet of clay. He will err but die a hero's death. In rebellion, if I narrated the battle, Grant would live with honor unblemished. But insofar as the morals of this fable are concerned, Admiral Grant's life or death is irrelevant.

Grant's putting himself at the heart of the decisive tactical action will be jarring and unrealistic to some readers, but it fulfills the longstanding naval tradition that a commander leads his forces from afloat. E. B. Potter, the eminent naval historian, said that on arrival at Pearl Harbor Admiral Nimitz only reluctantly decided that he would never be able to accompany his fleet to sea.[8] Nimitz had to stay ashore for access to sensitive intelligence and for freedom to communicate up and down the chain of command. Nimitz was going to lead a very long campaign. Grant does not have these problems, for his short campaign must result in one successful battle or fail. In that it is fair to predict that he will succeed; this is so in part because he is in the thick of it at the decisive point. But in most contemporary circumstances the fighting fleet is better served if the operational commander stays at headquarters while the tactical commander fights. Grant is nearly unique because I have embodied the requisite tactical skills in him.

A novelist would also tell us whether the American fleet's tactical victory led to successful negotiation and peace restored. I offer the reader no assurances about this. I can only assert that the president saw his best chance, the chairman of the Joint Chiefs gave the job to the best man, and American forces contributed everything that military action could do to give breathing room for negotiations.

A detailed description of the fighting would center on the *Cushings'* brave deception. The seven little combatants take on a force three times larger numerically and five times larger in displacement in order to draw some Turkish fangs. Neither side can do what every modern force armed with missiles wishes to do: stand off and deliver a decisive attack first. The battle is a purposeful melee, similar to the circumstances created by Rear Admiral Dan Callaghan (though probably inadvertently) in his night battle of Guadalcanal on 12–13 November 1942. Callaghan lost control but so confused both sides that one Japanese battleship was sunk and the other retreated. He died fulfilling his mission to protect Henderson Field at the climax of the campaign.

We saw in the previous chapter how to appraise the combat potential of two missile forces in opposition. We saw that if both sides are able to engage, the circumstances will be so unstable that a small change in the hit probabilities, the distribution of fire, defensive effectiveness, or the thwarted detection and tracking of all the enemy will create wide swings in the resulting damage. We saw why this was so and that the instability is inherent in missile warfare.

The only way to avoid the extreme uncertainty of outcome is to attack effectively first. A battle of exchange will be confused and unpredictable, yet Gridley's orders from Grant are to *force* an exchange. Despite coherent fighting instructions, after only a few salvoes he will lose control and the result will depend on the wits, discipline, and sangfroid in each *Cushing*. The same is true on the Turkish side. I have given the American side an edge in the first encounter (I don't know whether this is reasonable), but any application of the analytical technique in the previous chapter will conclude that the Turkish fleet can absorb an initial American success and still destroy the American force.

The Turks would fight differently if their purpose was simply to sink American ships. But the Turkish tactical commander has a higher responsibility to protect the beachhead, that is to say, to secure the safety of the amphibious operation. He must also husband his forces because the Greek navy lurks just beyond the metaphorical horizon. At the operational level it is almost always the case that a victory at sea is a means and not the end, and external considerations abound.

There is another reason I do not choose to narrate the night engagement by which Gridley will empower the *Phantoms'* attack. A narrative would imply too much power of tactical analysis to trace the probable course of events and foresee the outcome in detail. For what it is worth I calculate that the *Cushings* might be expected to take down (put out of action) an equal number of the enemy—about seven. I calculate that the Turkish fleet would expend a half of its 180 missiles in the confusion. The *Cushings* should expect to put more tonnage out of action and inflict more casualties because the enemy's ships are larger. If skillful in the opening moves, Gridley's seven corvettes might hit at most twelve enemy warships with the fifty-six Harpoons they carry. If the Turks are quick to react, they might suffer the loss of only three or four ships.

An interesting possibility is that countermeasures against the Harpoons are unexpectedly so successful that many ships are untouched after both sides' missiles are used up. The battle might conclude with gunfire. In a gunnery duel the Turkish force has a greater advantage still. Only the possibility of confusion could help the Americans to hurt and distract the Turks.

It is reasonable for Grant and Gridley to expect that when the battle is over few, if any, *Cushings* will limp away. Applying both the history of missile combat and the quantitative analysis in chapter 11, there is no way for the American

Cushings to defeat the Turkish battle force opposing them. The uncertainty of outcome is not *that* great. The Turkish fleet is quite competent, as are the coastal forces of many states when fighting in their home waters.

Gridley's *Cushings* are old ships similar to smaller, older combatants among most of the world's navies. The newness and the surprise are in the *Phantoms*. The *Phantoms'* TBMs, in combination with overhead sensors and a modern networked command and control system, comprise Grant's decisive combat system.

Though the circumstances of the Battle of the Aegean are unique, every battle in coastal waters will be unique. Many nations have well-conceived, tightly drawn, intensely practiced coastal defenses. In a more extended littoral conflict, land-based sensors, missiles, and aircraft will all be prominent. Depending on the geographical center of interest, coastal submarines and mines will be important. Based on the composition of coastal navies and their articulated strategies, small surface combatants, usually carrying missiles, will always participate. Coastal commercial vessels on the surface serving as scouts will also be important players. I believe to reduce casualties the U.S. Fleet must have numbers of small fighting ships that can be lost in combat without aborting a mission along a treacherous coast. It is for these reasons that I gave Grant the *Phantoms* and the *Cushings*. I do not think the existing American navy, even with all of its firepower, can fight unbloodied in the home waters of states with strong coastal defenses, including Turkey.

Notes

1. For a sound summary see Vlahos, "Wargaming." Also his *The Blue Sword*, an exhaustive study of the Naval War College's games during the same period.
2. Fourth-generation descendant of the captain of Dewey's flagship at Manila Bay in 1898.
3. This is a cavalier dismissal of a real choice, for much of the Turkish army is air-mobile. I set it aside because I have already painted what seems a sufficiently complicated operational situation to make the point that tactics attempt to reduce operational considerations to a simple and straightforward combat plan. Among the many American actions when an incipient air

movement was detected, one might be to insert the otherwise unemployed SEALs to perform their mischief at the airheads, which for fast turnaround Turkey would want near its west coast.

4. In his Naval Academy days Sammy (for Samarai) Genda was observed to be a master of creative mischief. He would never have survived to graduate if the Commandant had not persuaded the Superintendent that Sammy Genda's talents would someday bring rich rewards.

5. In Navy tradition tiny warships have carried names even when they cost only $60 million; stealthy U.S. Air Force bombers do not, even when they cost twenty times more.

6. In her veins flows the blood of the officer who, in the dead of night on 16 August 1804, cut out and burned the American frigate *Philadelphia* that had run aground and been captured by Tripolitanian pirates. Decatur was later killed in a duel. Stephanie having a temperament to match her ancestor, it is probably well that dueling is passe in her modern, more civilized navy.

7. Bernotti is the great-grandnephew of Romeo Bernotti, Italy's leading writer on the tactics and operations of his day. Ray has absorbed his ancestor's penchant for mathematical analysis as well as his familiarity with operations in the Mediterranean.

8. Potter, *The Battle of the Coral Sea*, in Sweetman, p. 244.

2 "THE MARINES WILL HAVE TO WALK"

(Selection from chapter 16 of *One Hundred Days*)

ADM Sandy Woodward, RN

Admiral Sir John "Sandy" Woodward was commander of the United Kingdom forces that first gained command of the sea in the South Atlantic and then took the Falkland Islands back, after Argentina had seized them in early April 1982. Written with the assistance of his coauthor Patrick Robinson, his memoir of the campaign is rich with the battles and tactics on the sea, in the air, and on the ground. It is the best and perhaps the only narrative by a tactical and operational commander in the missile era of combat at sea.

One Hundred Days describes most aspects of a modern campaign and its battles: air, submarine, amphibious, and land attacks, lacking only a battle between fleets of surface ships. His experience exemplifies the tense environment of modern combat. As you read, observe the constant alertness required and the danger of sudden attack. Observe the wide area in which the actions at sea take place. Although the vignette I have chosen from the book does not include the intense combat in the narrow waters in San Carlos Sound, *One Hundred Days* covers the successes and frustrations on both sides in fighting at the land-sea-air interface after the amphibious landings on 21 May 1982.

Also observe Woodward's disappointment with his warships' technologies, untested in combat, that didn't work as predicted from peacetime tests.

You will learn that constructing sound tactical formations for the Falklands War was as challenging as it was in 1942 when the U.S. Navy had to decide whether our carrier task forces should fight in single- or multi-carrier task groups. On the complex issue of formation design, I invite your attention to the Argentine attack by two Super Etendards carrying Exocet missiles. The attacking pilots hoped to hit and damage one of the Royal Navy's two aircraft carriers. The Exocets failed in their purpose because they homed on the first ship they saw, HMS *Ambuscade.* She was a screening ship intended to protect the high-value ships in the formation. A problem arose that had never been seen before. The *Ambuscade* did what tactical doctrine taught: she released chaff to draw off the missiles and thus saved herself. When the two missiles went for the chaff and missed the destroyer, they sought another target and, lo, there in front of them was the big supply ship, *Atlantic Conveyer*, full of critical stores and carrying the heavy lift helicopters intended to transport the forces on the ground across East Falkland Island. The missiles struck and destroyed her. By saving herself *Ambuscade* failed in her purpose to protect a vital ship from harm. Formation configuration is still an important part of tactics.

"THE MARINES WILL HAVE TO WALK"

(Selection from chapter 16 of *One Hundred Days: The Memoirs of the Falklands Battle Group Commander*) by ADM Sandy Woodward, RN (Naval Institute Press, 1992): 290–300.

The loss of HMS *Coventry*, the last of my original picket ships, weighed heavily upon me. I had lost an old and familiar friend. I stood once more alone in the glass-fronted Admiral's Bridge on that desolate afternoon staring out over the cold Atlantic, watching the always-busy deck of *Hermes* and cursing the world in general. Cursing specifically Argentina and her bloody National Day. It was *still* 25 May, as it had been, it seemed to me, for about the last thousand hours. I glanced at my watch. It was a little after 1900Z, still another couple of hours of daylight left, and then several hours of uncertain darkness before it became, with any luck, 26 May.

I gazed at the sea, and pondered the many times I had stood here before; times when I had searched my own soul, wondering whether I should send the quietly spoken David Hart-Dyke into the most lethal spot on this most lethal southern ocean. Well, I suppose I had done it once too often and now the gallant *Coventry* was gone—small comfort for her captain to know that she had gone down fighting, in a manner which had conferred the greatest credit upon his crew and indeed had done his illustrious family proud. Doubtless as I stood there, he was resting in *Broadsword*, alone as he will always be, with the terrible visions of the last moments of his ship, of the fires, of the screams of the burning men, of lost friends, of the darkness and the helplessness. I doubt if it will ever be entirely erased from his sub-conscious, though in moments of sadness, he may perhaps find solace in the heroism and the selflessness demonstrated by the young men who fought with him, to the end. There is an aura of lasting, private glory about such disasters, understood, inevitably, only by those who were actually there.

In the last chapter I tried to concentrate the events of the day from the point of view of the ships which fought the action. But there is no doubt that from first light I had had a very distinct premonition that this was going to be an especially depressing few hours. I began my diary right after breakfast with an irritable diatribe about the weather, bemoaning our luck that since the landings, four days previously, we had been sitting out here under almost clear skies. Today we were in a slowly clearing fog, but it was bright over the mainland— the worst possible combination for us.

The bad visibility around us should clear at about midday. The Args seldom arrive before 1300, so all may yet be well. Again though, the question arises of whether to take the carriers west into non-AAR range [Navy shorthand for an area where the Args fighter-bombers can reach us without having to refuel in the air]. My answer, reinforced by our lack of escorts, is [again] no.

I have with us only two Type 21s, one Type 42, and one DLG [*Glamorgan*] (useless really), and *Brilliant* (not very fit). *Coventry* is up front in the missile trap with *Broadsword*. *Glasgow* is de-storing to the rear. *Bristol* won't be here till midnight and *Cardiff* is even further behind. COMAW is still unprepared to rely on Rapier and I can't say I blame him. Missile trap needed for better CAP direction meanwhile.

1200. This has all the signs of a disastrous day. COMAW has packed the stage with ships he can't possibly unload today, the "missile trap" is in clear sky, and the carriers are in thick fog. Combat air patrol cannot be provided. The only thing to be thankful for is that this did not happen on Day One. And the only hope is that the Args have had enough for the moment, and perhaps their minds are on other things.

1300. It cleared and the CAP is up. Thank Heavens.

1600. The reports from the Amphibious Operating Area and the missile trap are various, but it sounds as though the Args have been into Carlos Water with A4s [Skyhawks] and Pucaras and lost several. At about 1900 yet another bloody disaster. Three A4s apparently trundled in towards AOA over Pebble Island, swerved north, and bombed *Coventry* and *Broadsword*. *Coventry* badly hit and sinking. *Broadsword* probably not too badly, picking up survivors. No missiles fired—which is quite extraordinary and saps any faith we may have had in our modern systems, even against these previous-generation [Arg] aircraft.

Looking back all of these years later I realize that it was a terrible moment for me. One of those times when a commander has no one to whom he can turn, for fear of betraying uncertainty or wavering will-power. But I remember thinking to myself, "Christ! Where are we? Are we actually *losing* this?" It was, without any question, thus far my lowest ebb of the whole operation. I walked back into my cabin and sat for a while alone. I opened my notebook and jotted down a few notes in the following coldly pessimistic mood:

1. The 42/22 combination does not work.
2. Sea Dart virtually useless against low fliers.
3. Sea Wolf unreliable.
4. Surface ships have to have Airborne Early Warning and Combat Air Patrol up-threat for survival in open water.
5. We must do much more rigorous multi-target trials of Anti-Air War systems.
6. Stick to night operations and/or bad weather.
7. They really must try to come for the carriers now!

That did not take me long and I went once more back out to the bridge, hoping that the view of the sea and sky would somehow clear my mind and allow my perspective and sense of clarity to return. I stood there for several minutes pondering our formation, pondering the likelihood of another Arg strike before dark.

At this moment *Hermes* was about four miles up-threat from *Invincible*, more or less due north. John Coward in the improving *Brilliant* was keeping "goal" for us and, ranged in a north-south line facing west, the fleet auxiliaries formed what I hoped was some kind of a "chaff" wall in case of incoming threat. In the most brutal terms, I could afford to lose a big merchant ship, or even a tanker, a whole lot more than I could afford to lose a carrier—not that I thought very highly of either option. It was simply a matter of the lesser of two evils. Anyway, out in front I did have the newly arrived *Exeter* with her sharp Captain Hugh Balfour and her Sea Dart system with all the latest improvements.

The only area which I did find rather worrying was the position of the *Atlantic Conveyor*, stationed by me at the far north end of the line of the auxiliaries, on the "disengaged" side from Rio Grande, home of the Etendards. This 18,000-ton Cunard roll-on-roll-off freighter was of incalculable value to us, for she still carried three of the big troop transport helicopters, the Chinooks (these priceless monsters can lift twelve tons) and five Wessex. She already had one Chinook and one Wessex in the air and had brought down the Atlantic from England fourteen Harriers wrapped in plastic bags and lashed down to her upper deck. They had been unwrapped, serviced, and flown off as soon as *Conveyor* reached the Battle Group, of course, and were a critically important reinforcement for our dwindling Harrier force.

Atlantic Conveyor had two landing spots on her long "flight deck." Since her arrival several days ago she had been used virtually as a third aircraft carrier by the chopper pilots. She was still loaded to the gunwales with stores and ammunition including six hundred cluster bombs for the Harriers and *all* of the equipment we needed to construct an airstrip for Harriers in the beachhead area in Carlos Water. Her refitting, loading, and preparation in Devonport had been a masterpiece of organization and in her cargo holds were most of the spares and support equipment for the land force helicopters. Her captain was a real old sea dog named Ian North, a Yorkshireman who had been twice sunk during the Second World War. All the way south from Liverpool he had made himself increasingly popular with the young seamen in his ship from both branches of the Navy, regaling them with stories of the sea and occasionally, late at night, to the delight of everyone, playing his trombone. When they "crossed the line," the short, chunky Ian North, with his snowy beard, played the part, inevitably, of King Neptune.

The senior Royal Naval officer on board, Captain Mike Layard (now a rear admiral) adored the old boy, for his humour, his complete professionalism, and for his wisdom. He also admired him for his philosophical outlook, remembering that Captain North was probably the only senior officer who actually *knew* what it was like to be hit, possibly the only man in the entire operation who had no illusions about what to expect in the event of a bomb, missile or torpedo strike. Between them Captain Layard and Captain North made a just-about-perfect team. Indeed on a quick visit to *Hermes* a few days previously Captain Layard could not resist telling me of an incident which took place as they flew the tenth Harrier off the deck, vertically, for the short flight over to the carriers.

The pilot mistakenly had the jet nozzles facing slightly aft as well as down and when he opened up the throttle to lift off, the aircraft charged across the deck straight towards the guard rails. The pilot, with well-honed instinct for survival, slammed the nozzles to the vertical and the Harrier leaped into the air, clearing the guard rails with inches to spare. Men were already rushing for cover, but Captain North turned to Captain Layard and said, deadpan, "Hmmmm. That's rather a novel way of doing it."

We had deliberately retained the *Conveyor* back in the holding area until the very last moment, until the timing was exactly right for them to make a fast run into Carlos Water, unload as much as possible overnight with all speed, then get the hell out of there and back to the relative safety of the Battle Group. Well, tonight was the night and it had seemed reasonable to me to bring them forward into the Battle Group two hours early, exposing them to some small risk of air attack for a few daylight hours, but granting them more hours to unload in the dark. My alternative was to leave them in complete safety until dark, east of the Battle Group, and then let them run late into the AOA with the prospect of either a dangerous return trip in broad daylight or of spending the whole of the next day inshore in "Bomb Alley." Bearing in mind the fact that the Args had not launched a successful raid on the deep-water Battle Group out here since *Sheffield* was hit three weeks ago today, it seemed to me that the dark hours in Carlos Water were worth playing for . . . especially as the *Conveyor* would be in ten times *more* danger parked in the Sound tomorrow morning possibly in bright sunlight—the quintessential sitting duck.

And so, earlier that morning I had ordered *Atlantic Conveyor* into the Battle Group, taking the precaution of stationing her at the likely "safe" end of the line of auxiliaries while she waited for the light to fade before beginning her dark journey inshore. Captain North and Captain Layard had already ordered their white super-structure to be painted a dark matt grey for the hundred-mile voyage. Understandably, tension in the big container ship was extremely high; everyone preparing to make the last lap of the highly dangerous task with which they had been charged.

However, unknown to any of us, as I had pondered the world and made my notes, two Argentinian Etendards were making a long sweep north up from Rio Grande before heading slightly south of east for their final approach towards the

Battle Group. They had gone a very long way out of their direct route in order to surprise us by coming in from the north-west. They had been refuelled and now, just as I returned to my cabin for the second time, shortly after 1830, they "popped up" to look for us. They were about forty miles out. *Exeter* promptly detected their radars on her UAA1 ESM, and issued a formal warning to the rest of the Battle Group. Within the minute, *Ambuscade* picked them up on her own radar at twenty-four miles and *Brilliant*, further back, "saw" them at twenty-eight miles. Roars of "CHAFF!" echoed through the Ops Rooms. At 1838 the two Argentinians released their Exocets, both at the same "blip," the first they came across—Commander Peter Mosse's Type 21 frigate *Ambuscade*, from which the chaff rockets had already been launched. The two French-built missiles swerved past her and hurtled through the chaff cloud, deceived but still looking ahead for a target.

Which they immediately found. They each adjusted course automatically to skim the water for another four miles straight towards *Atlantic Conveyor*. On board the freighter they had no chaff. Mike Layard, upon receipt of the "Air Raid Warning Red" signal, had given the order to broadcast instantly *"Emergency stations! Emergency stations!"* The ship's siren was blasting out its deafening "BAAHA . . . BAAHA . . . BAAHA" and everyone with a gun was heading for the upper deck. Machine-gun crews were at action stations on each wing of the bridge, complete with aimers, loaders, and lookouts. All damage-control and first-aid parties took up their posts. Anyone without a specific task headed for the two dining rooms to act as man-power pools in case of serious damage. Everyone was pulling on life-jackets and anti-flash gear as they ran to their places of duty. Captain Layard took the steps to the bridge three at a time. Captain North had ordered a hard turn to port in an attempt to present *Conveyor*'s very strong stern to the incoming missiles. At 1841 Captain Layard demanded the threat direction, but even as he did so both Exocets crashed through *Atlantic Conveyor*'s port quarter—nine feet above the waterline—with an enormous explosion.

Sir Percivale and Christopher Craig's *Alacrity* were quickly on their way to help, and Captain North's fire-fighting crews were struggling with a rare desperation to contain the blaze. They activated the water sprinkler systems, tried to blanket the fires with carbon dioxide gas, shut down all the ventilation fans, and pumped sea water through all the fire hoses they could find down into the cargo decks. But it was all hopeless. The ship rapidly filled with acrid black smoke, just as *Sheffield* had. The whole of the upper deck was becoming too hot to stand on and the fire was creeping forward towards thousands of gallons of kerosene and the huge consignment of cluster bombs. The *Atlantic Conveyor* was one massive explosion waiting to happen. Eleven men were already dead.

Captain Layard conferred with the Master of the merchant ship at 1920 and in Captain North's opinion there was no alternative but to abandon her. *Atlantic Conveyor* was doomed and so was her precious cargo of helicopters, as were the proposed landing strip at the beach-head and all the spares. The land forces were going to have to walk across East Falkland.

Meanwhile *Invincible* picked up yet another pair of solid contacts only twenty miles out, heading for *Hermes*. She launched *six* Sea Dart missiles in short order, adding to the confusion on the radar screens of the entire force, before it all turned out to be spurious. The consensus in *Hermes* was that *Invincible* had been shooting at our chaff blooms—certainly the sky had filled with ordnance of one kind or another, little of it being of Arg origin.

Back in *Atlantic Conveyor* there was no good news whatsoever. One team of thirteen fire-fighters were cut off and trapped, but we got them off with a Sea King from *Hermes*. The remainder of the one hundred and thirty-four men would have to climb down the ladders and ropes into the life rafts, a task which would become nightmarish because of the explosions inside the ship. Parts of the hull were now glowing red hot in the gathering dark. But somehow they managed, and finally Captain Layard set off, the second last man to leave. Behind him, close to exhaustion, climbed Captain Ian North, who, at sixty-ish, was perhaps least able to cope with this awful physical test.

Mike dropped the last ten feet into the icy water. Ian North splashed in beside him. But something was wrong. He was floating too low in the water. The Royal Navy officer grabbed him by the life jacket, holding him up, but the *Conveyor*, with her rounded stern, was riding up and down in the long swell. As she rose, she sucked the men in, under the overhang, before falling down on top of them, forcing them beneath the surface. "My God!" muttered Captain Layard. "She's going to take us to the bottom with her."

Within minutes the great heaving freighter had sucked in the life rafts which were squashing the men against the ship's side, a terrifying experience, especially for the several non-swimmers who found it difficult enough just to breathe. But Mike Layard hung on to Ian North until finally he got a hand on a life raft. He summoned all of his remaining strength and shoved the old captain in the small of the back, straight at the raft, but the sea broke over them. Captain Layard went under, grabbing for Ian North, but when the Royal Navy officer came up there was no sign of the Master of the *Conveyor*. With frantic courage Captain Layard dived after him.

But Ian North was gone, claimed by the great sea he had been plying all of his working life. Mike Layard surfaced again half drowned, grabbed at another man in trouble and swam with him to the raft, from which hands reached down and heaved them aboard. The captain passed out after that and it was several minutes before they could revive him. When he did regain consciousness he could only see the bright orange glow of the burning Cunarder and he sat with his head in his hands and wept for his friend, Captain Ian North. The trauma stayed with him for a long time too. Thirteen days later when he arrived back in England they had arranged a press conference, but it had to be delayed for half an hour because Captain Layard couldn't bear it, unable to speak for the lump in his throat. It's often that way with the bravest of men.

Meanwhile there was still enormous danger in the life rafts as the rising stern kept sucking them in towards her, then, falling again, threatening to squash them. Not for the first time completely regardless of his own safety, Commander Christopher Craig, minesweeper extraordinary, brought *Alacrity* right up to the floating time-bomb which was the *Conveyor*—she would surely have taken them *both* to the bottom if she had exploded—and fired lifelines over to the rafts. Then gently, he backed his ship away and towed them all clear.

By now I was back out on my bridge and I could see the *Atlantic Conveyor* burning on the horizon. I watched her, on and off, until she disappeared in the dark distance and wondered, without much genuine optimism, if they could save anything, if we could get a salvage party on board and reclaim some of her precious equipment. But the following morning she was just a dangerous, drifting hulk as another internal explosion blew her bow off. Her war had lasted exactly thirty days and, even without her final mission accomplished, we still owed her a considerable debt. Not least, I suppose, because she was in a dead line between *Hermes* and *Ambuscade*. If the *Conveyor* had possessed a chaff system and decoyed the missiles, they might have come straight on for the carrier. We may, or may not, have been able to divert them yet again.

Conveyor's loss left the Land Forces very badly placed for any means of transport other than walking to get from Carlos to Stanley. And it left me assailed by guilt—again. Was it all my fault? Had I just made a horrendous mistake? Should I have left her safely to the east of the Battle Group until dark? Who knows? I suppose if I had waited and let her go in late and the Args had blown her apart with bombs the following morning, everyone would have assumed automatically that I was off my head for not getting her in there earlier and on her way home by dawn. You can't win, as ever. Sad and troubled as I was, I resolved once more to put it behind me and to press on.

I sat down to finish my diary, and saw that it was still not quite midnight. "Sod it!" I said to myself bitterly. "It's *still* 25 May. Will this bloody day ever end?" In the late afternoon I had felt fairly certain this was the worst day of my life. Now I was sure of it. My diary paragraph, as always, reflected my despondency by being as dry as dust, as if I were trying to write the emotion out of it. "Half an hour later two Etendards got in amongst the Battle Group—actually detected on radar in good time, like at twenty-four miles from *Ambuscade*, twenty-eight miles by *Brilliant*, and even in *Hermes*, visually by all. Seduced by *Ambuscade*'s chaff and went for *Atlantic Conveyor*—both hit, well aft. *Conveyor* a total loss, but eighty per cent of crew saved and one Chinook and one Wessex 5. Down goes another £100 million worth. The Etendards got away, having fired at the first thing they saw."

As if my half-morbid, half-furious mood were not enough, there was yet another serious cause for anger circulating the Ops Rooms of Operation Corporate. You will doubtless recall that several of the bombs which hit the British ships in Carlos Water had, happily for us, not exploded, thus saving a considerable number of lives. Well, on the evening of 23 May—forty-eight hours ago—the BBC, in the light of information from the MOD, announced this. Not content with broadcasting it locally in London, for the ears of any Argentinian diplomat or military attaché, they actually put it out on the World Service for the entire South Atlantic to hear. Some of my officers were outraged and their anger was fuelled by the inescapable coincidence that all three bombs which had hit *Coventry* had exploded. Of course the Args *may* have sorted out the fusing problems on their own, but that could not stop much hostile comment about "shallow, smug, half-educated morons who work at the BBC." As you can imagine, since the BBC World Service was the sole source of media information to us, we were less than delighted.

I realized their self-appointed task as "Fearless Seekers After Truth" was, to them, sacrosanct. But their "ratings" that week just may have been paid for with the blood of Captain Hart-Dyke's people. This ought to have upset me too, but I couldn't allow myself to be put off balance by this sort of thing—for me, it could only be classified as "spilt milk." And, for all I knew, the information had been given to the BBC by the MOD anyway. While it was clear that something *must* be done by someone about this sort of carelessness, it was unlikely to be me.

Finally, 25 May ended. The new early morning saw me, as I had been so often, sitting by myself in my cabin, putting yesterday behind me and trying to formulate my thoughts for the immediate future. I began by revising my "Lessons"—they were fairly rough notes, so I have added occasional words for clarification here.

1. Radar *will* detect and track aircraft and missiles at reasonable range.
2. Chaff *can* seduce [Exocet], off small ships [*Ambuscade*] anyway.
3. Using merchant vessels as spare targets probably not such a good idea—unless they [also] have chaff.
4. Remember UAA1 distribution for the screen [picket line]. OK this time, but more by accident [. . . than design].
5. Keep escorts fairly well forward for early warning.

6. Do not have too many ships, in depth, down Anti-Air Warfare axis otherwise missile [Exocet] has too many chances to get it right.

7. Stay outside 460-mile circles [from Arg mainland air bases]; we'd had to creep inside for CAP [over AOA].

8. Turn towards [incoming missiles]. At least you present the strongest part of the ship that way.

9. [To find the escaping Etendards] Fire [send] CAP straight out along the initial bearing [of Handbrake warning]. Opposition will be scampering low out along it.

10. Cross fingers.

Beneath these notes I wrote the words: "And so the war will go on. Setbacks, yes. Defeat, no. But we are very much in need of a decent airfield ashore."

3 "TACTICAL DEVELOPMENT"

CDR Frank A. Andrews, USN

Frank Andrews' brilliant essay offers concise and pointed advice for developing better tactics in peacetime. He wrote at a time when the combat lessons of World War II needed major adjustment due to technological advancements, the rise of the Soviet Union, and the need for a fleet that could be distributed around the world to prevent or constrain small wars. He shows that better tactics have always come from (1) blending new technology and different operations, while (2) recognizing that the enemy has a vote in how and where a battle will be fought. He emphasizes the frequently overlooked importance of the environment, both as it is affected by the weather on, above, and below the ocean surface and as it is influenced by geography and ocean traffic. Today we must put more emphasis on the land side as well, because ever since the development of long-range Soviet bombers the land is now a major source of combat potential that expands the significance of the tactical maxim "A ship's a fool to fight a fort."

Captain Andrews went on to practice what he preached as commodore of Submarine Development Group Two in New London where, in the early 1960s, he was one of a series of superb leaders who developed submarine tactics to defeat the rising Soviet submarine threat.

The SubDevGru blended operations analysis, knowledge of physics, and exercises at sea to achieve what were probably the most effective single-unit tactics of any branch of any navy during the Cold War.

While leading the SubDevGru, Andrews played a central role in locating USS *Thresher* (SSN 593) after she went down east of Boston in April 1963 and in determining the probable cause. He became an expert in search theory and participated in finding USS *Scorpion* (SSN 589) and other important things on the ocean floor.

Young Ensign Andrews acquired an early appreciation for the need of good tactics when he twice was on board destroyers sunk in World War II, one off Guadalcanal and one in the Mediterranean. But most of his career was in submarines or devoted to advancements in submarine technology and tactics.

"TACTICAL DEVELOPMENT"

By CDR Frank A. Andrews, USN, U.S. Naval Institute *Proceedings* (April 1958): 65–73.

Between wars a great many thoughts are conceived and a great many words are written on strategy. Some will redefine the term. Some will categorize the term, breaking national strategy into military, economic, and foreign strategy. And all will examine wars of the past to show that the principles of Mahan, Douhet, or Clausewitz, or some other equally famous writer on strategy were correctly or incorrectly or never applied.

Not so often, however, does one see a detailed treatise in popular or even professional publications on the subject of tactics. This is very likely as it should be, when one considers that tactics are more in the nature of the detailed plans of carrying out strategy; hence, the sort of ideas that will occur more readily to the operator at sea, and, further, of the sort which one would be very wise to keep from any potential enemy.

As a matter of fact, the big names associated with the principles of sea power, air power, or land warfare are relatively easy for any military student to pick out. But who can name the man who first conceived naval dive bombing, or the ahead-throwing weapon attack on submarines, or the submarine night-surface approach on a convoy?

This paper then starts with a two-fold assumption. First, that military strategy is the broad plan for waging a war, cold or hot; and second, that tactics are the details of battle in which the commander faces an adversary.

The Element of Tactics

First, then, what are the elements of tactics? Before answering this question, let us look at certain obvious facts concerning the physical world about us. It is, in part, a material world, in which the action carried out by, through, and on material has an all important significance. Simply stated, one cannot separate how one acts from the wherewithal with which one acts. To move a mountain has only part of a meaning. To move a mountain with a hand shovel has a complete meaning, and a meaning totally different from moving a mountain with a hydrogen bomb. In like manner, it is impossible to discuss tactics without completing the picture by defining the kind of hardware assumed.

Recently an idea has been introduced into the U.S. Navy, called the "Weapon System" concept. This concept would have us no longer think of the effectiveness of one ship versus another, or of one detection system versus another, or of one weapon versus another weapon. Rather we are asked to view the ship, its detection system, and its weapon as an entity, a complete weapon system. Thus we see a system of mutually dependent parts, in which a poor ship might be offset by an outstanding weapon, or an outstanding detection system might be rendered completely ineffective because of a poor weapon.

This writer would ask you to go one step further and think not just of a Weapon System, but rather of a "Weapon System Operation," which for brevity's sake will be shortened to "Weapon-Operation." He would then suggest that battles are fought by your Weapon-Operation, over which you have control, against the enemy's Weapon-Operation, over which the enemy has control. And these battles are fought in the natural world of sea, storm, and darkness about us over which only God has control. The elements of tactics then are shown in Figure 1.

By way of illustration, consider the World War II "ASW destroyer-depth charge-searchlight sonar" weapon system. To say it is or was, or would still be effective against submarines is a meaningless statement. As a matter of fact, it is of interest to see how many wardroom arguments start just this way. The debate proceeds for fifteen minutes before the two participants settle down to introduce the missing elements of this tactical or Weapon-Operation discussion. They then decide to narrow the argument by considering:

a.   The World War II "ASW destroyer-depth charge-searchlight sonar" weapon system, plus

b.   The assumption that this hardware has picked up a sonar contact while sailing in a convoy screen in

c.   Natural surroundings such as daylight, isothermal sonar conditions, and mild sea state against

d.   The contact, which is in actual fact a type VII German U-boat, plus

e.   A skipper who is attempting screen penetration at periscope depth, and who has decided to fire a high speed, straight running torpedo at any escort who closes to within 500 yards.

Figure 1: The Elements of Tactics

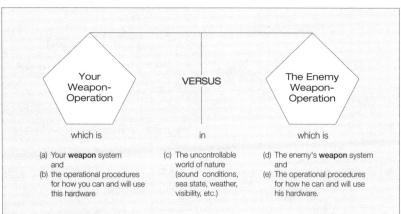

Once all the elements are introduced, the discussion can progress more intelligently, but until that time the two debaters can easily be talking in entirely different ball parks.

Starting then with a Weapon-Operation as the basis for bringing destruction to the enemy, which is after all the end product for which a military must seek in wartime, let us examine the paths through which tactical development makes progress.

Paths for Tactical Improvement

Essentially, two ways are available. First, the capability of the Weapon System can be improved, and second, the operational procedures for using the Weapon System can be improved.

The mark of Weapon System improvement is new hardware with increased capability. A multitude of examples exist from World War II, or any war for that matter. From World War I, the introduction of the submarine and the airplane remind us of vast tactical changes brought by these two new items of hardware. From World War II, radar as a new detection device; the carrier as a new ship type; the homing torpedo, the glide bomb, the ahead-throwing ASW projectile as new weapons; the snorkel; and the bigger submarine battery as a new twist to an old vehicle; the various amphibious landing craft; and other material changes, *ad infinitum*, brought about new tactics unheard of in battle before this war.

On the other hand, the mark of operational procedure change is some new way of using the old hardware. As an example, one sees the World War II German U-boats unable to close targets because of the submarines' limited endurance and extremely slow speed (four to five knots) while submerged. To solve this tactical problem, the German skippers, under cover of darkness, surfaced their boats, not only to charge batteries, but also to close aggressively and attack their prey as high speed (seventeen to eighteen knots) surface torpedo boats. The greater surface endurance and higher speed coupled with the submarine's low silhouette and darkness gave the U-boat such maneuverability and speed advantage over the large bulky Allied convoys that, literally, groups of thirty to forty ships were torn to shreds. The wholesale installation of radar on Allied ships and airplanes finally put a stop to this, but not before the German surfaced submarine attack had created tremendous damage to the Allied merchant navy.

The use of destroyer-escorts in the hunter-killer group represents another World War II change in operational procedure resulting in tactical improvement. As a matter of interest, the question of whether to concentrate escorts in the screen around a convoy, or whether to order several escorts away as a hunter-killer team to close U-boats sighted miles ahead of the convoy, caused serious and heated debate amongst our own and British naval officers at the beginning of World War II. The book, *Walker, R.N.* describes in detail the part the famous British anti-submariner, Captain Walker, Royal Navy, played at the beginning of the British War in developing and proving the destroyer hunter-killer concept, and thus, incidentally, solving the problem of what tactics to use with an ASW destroyer.

Originally, of course, the ASW destroyer was conceived as operating in a screen directly around the convoy. One school argued that the defense of the convoy was the all important consideration, hence under no circumstances should destroyers be detached from the screen. The other school argued that the submarine sighted miles ahead by an airplane, or located by radio direction finder ahead of the convoy, was a known and positive contact, therefore of greater danger than some possible contact nearer the convoy, but which had not even been determined to exist. The later, more aggressive tactics of closing to kill any and all positive submarine contacts finally proved itself the more effective.

Other examples of operational procedure change exist in great number. The battleship, the cruiser, and the destroyer were used as artillery to back up amphibious landings; the submarine was used as a life guard for air strikes; the carrier was used as a floating air field to bring small aircraft to battle submarines at sea. Each of these was a new way of using the old hardware.

Up to this point, then, two notions have been formulated. First, tactics must be viewed in terms of a Weapon-Operation. Second, tactical changes come about either through a change in the Weapon System or a change in the operational procedures for using a Weapon System, or both.

A Superior Weapon-Operation

Once these two ideas are incorporated into one's thinking, other pertinent thoughts on tactics and tactical development soon follow.

Battles are not necessarily won by superior weapons, nor do inferior weapons necessarily guarantee defeat. But rather the outcome of battle hinges on a superior Weapon-Operation. Better guns, better ships, better radar can easily be penalized by poorly trained crews, poorly formulated operational procedures, or unimaginative, unaggressive actions which the enemy can see are developing hours before an engagement takes place. Fletcher Pratt in *Battles That Changed History* points out that Lord Horatio Nelson's success at both the Nile and at Trafalgar were battles of roughly equal forces, but ones also in which aggressiveness was keynoted by Nelson's statement to his captains, his "band of brothers," that "No captain can go far wrong who lays his ship alongside the enemy."

Both of these battles also demonstrated the genius of the tactician, Nelson, who somehow contrived to maneuver two British ships alongside of each of one-half the French force, while the other half of the French force was out of position and hence had nobody to fight.

At the Battle of Midway, on the other hand, Admirals Spruance and Fletcher were outnumbered by four Japanese carriers to three American carriers, one of which was the carrier *Yorktown*, not completely repaired from damage received at the Coral Sea battle. And yet because the American forces were not supposed to be at Midway, by Japanese estimates; were not supposed to be able to attack the Japanese carriers, by Japanese estimates; the American planes *did* attack the Japanese carriers while the Japanese planes were either down from a strike on Midway, or still returning. Clearly, this was a victory because the American forces wanted it so and worked for it.

As a matter of fact, in battle, there is no requirement that a Weapon-Operation be good or bad, only that it be better than that possessed by the enemy. One can see that given two pieces of war hardware which are roughly on a par, such as a submarine versus a destroyer, or a carrier task force versus an air-defended land mass, or a surface ship versus another surface ship, the victor will be determined only by the outcome of the clash between the minds and the wills of the two opposing commanding officers. Furthermore, given hardware of an inferior capability, for example, a ship of slower speed, a submarine with poorer torpedoes, or a carrier with fewer planes, the tide of battle can still be swung by a commanding officer whose operational procedures embody the correct elements of surprise, aggression, concentration of effort, imagination, courage, and all the other many and pertinent characteristics which always distinguish the way one person more than another successfully accomplishes an aim in this life.

Unfortunately, a nation cannot afford to be too inferior in hardware as compared to its enemy, because there may not be enough outstanding commanding officers to offset the superior hardware of the enemy. The loss by the Japanese of so many good naval carrier pilots at the Battle of Midway is often given as step one in the final defeat of the Japanese carrier navy. In like manner, there is no doubt that the German U-boat arm in 1943 and 1944 was fighting its Atlantic battle with mere babes for skippers in comparison to the 1939–1940 years.

And so it goes. The few brilliant leaders may win a few battles by outstanding personal performance, but the war, which is composed of many battles, may be lost because the majority of good, but only average, leaders are overwhelmed in battle by superior enemy hardware.

On the other hand, when the tide of war is running favorably, the brilliant leaders can do more than a lion's share of the damage. In the book *By Guess and By God*, a story of British submarines in World War I, by Mr. W. G. Carr, the preface written by Admiral S. S. Hall R.N. reports this interesting fact: "During World War I, Germany had some 400 submarine captains, but over sixty per cent of the U-boat success was accomplished by but twenty-two of these four hundred officers."

Obviously success is guaranteed by good hardware and good leaders. But what happens so often is that all the first line nations become relatively equal in hardware capability during the peace time years preceding a war. Witness the capability of the German submarines or the Japanese carriers at the onset of World War II. Then the outcome of battles is determined by one thing alone—who has the best commanding officers?

Hardware Changes Slowly

The second thought on tactics and tactical development arising from considering battles fought by a Weapon-Operation is this: The hardware which makes up a weapon system changes with painful slowness. On the other hand, operational procedures can change at the snap of the finger of a capable commanding officer.

The reason for the slow production of hardware is a fact of life. To build planes, and ships, and bullets requires men, and material, and hours. A nation's pool of men is just so large, and hence great demands on the nation for many different types of military hardware can only be furnished in time. Today, in 1958, a U.S. submarine requires three years to construct, a destroyer three years, and a carrier four years. Naturally, in wartime this might be accomplished faster, if the building yards were free from enemy bombardment. New types of weapons such as guided missiles, or anti- and pro-submarine torpedoes, require not only long periods of time for production, but also must go through a lengthy design, prototype development, and operational checkout phase before they even get into production. Small wonder then that although the Press may play up a new and different piece of naval hardware, many years go by before the Fleet is completely equipped with it.

The operational procedures for current hardware, on the other hand, are a different story. Within the performance capabilities of various weapon systems, we see that a commanding officer can do as he pleases, when he pleases. It therefore follows that if a particular tactical problem arises in peacetime during training against one's own forces, or in wartime when engaging the enemy, the quickest road to success is to seek for new tactics by changing operation procedures.

This point is usually quite obvious in wartime, because the wartime commanding officer is playing for keeps. In peacetime, the situation may differ in that a hit by the opposition does not carry the same disastrous result. One can easily check off the lack of success in peacetime exercises to poorer weapons, and merrily sail for port and the officer's club. Then, when the exercise critique comes along, one simply screams loudly for better weapons. The new hardware may one day arrive, but in the meanwhile quick success might be at hand through a new way of using the old hardware. In fact, an over-developed preoccupation with the new hardware yet to come is without doubt one of the mental burdens which the present day naval Officer carries around.

Moreover, implicit in these above statements is the obligation of a commanding officer; in war, to do the best he can with the hardware he has, because he can be sure there will not be any new types furnished during the battle; in peace, to train himself to do the best he can with the hardware he has, because this is the challenge he will face in wartime.

In addition, of course, while learning to get along with what is at hand, the commanding officer must conscientiously seek after the production of new and better hardware. However, he must never count on fighting his future battles with hardware he hasn't yet received. The war may arrive, and the hardware may not.

Interestingly, the commanding officer, when he views his obligations to his country, sits squarely on the horns of a dilemma. On the one hand, he must do the best he can with what he has. This naturally requires a great deal of optimism on his part. On the other hand, he is at fault if he presents a falsely optimistic view to the procurers of his new hardware, for then new hardware may be even more tardy. In these matters, the best course undoubtedly is for the commanding officer to view himself as a private citizen and ask only for what he sincerely feels that his country realistically needs.

The Enemy Must Use What He Has

The third thought derived from viewing the weapon system and its operation in combination is this. The hardware which an enemy possesses will, in all probability, be used. But by contrast, the operational procedures which he has worked out in peacetime may or may not be used. This thought is allied to the thought above that material is gathered and forged into weapon hardware at great cost to a nation, hence this hardware obviously must be used somehow when war comes to that nation. Operational procedures, on the other hand, can still be changed by the forthright and imaginative thinking of a capable commanding officer, enemy or not.

Furthermore, an enemy's operational procedures, like our own, are formulated not so much on what will be used in a future war, but rather on these:

(a) What his own forces do in peacetime exercises against him. For example, our peacetime submarine commanding officers are faced day by day with the tactics of our own ASW forces. This is true of the Russians, the British, or anybody else. Hence our operating procedures are apt to concentrate more on competing with these brother units than with the unknown tactics of an enemy not yet engaged. Indeed, one very important reason for the Russian buildup of a sizeable surface navy may be to provide sparring partners for their mammoth submarine force.

(b) What his own forces did in some past war against some enemy whom he may never fight again. Thus, as example taken from our own Navy, our carrier forces will naturally retain certain operational procedures developed in the past world war against Japanese carriers in the Pacific and against German submarines in the Atlantic. That this is so makes sense, since memories of those past battles are still fresh in the minds of officers still serving in the present day carriers.

Hence, when new enemies meet, it is inevitable that the hardware available at war's commencement must be used; it is likewise inevitable that the operational procedures will change radically.

This last statement contains a most important implication, which, perhaps, can best be brought out by this example. Suppose one views the size of the present Russian submarine arm, reportedly on the order of 450 to 500 boats, and compares that with the size of the German U-boat arm at the beginning of World War II, thirty boats, or with the maximum number of boats which the Germans had available at the very apex of their success in the Battle of the Atlantic, some 300 boats. One might then argue that because of the overwhelming Russian submarine fleet, because many of these boats have characteristics similar to the deep diving, higher submerged speed, snorkel German Type XXI boat, and because the quantity (not necessarily the quality) of our own ASW forces are diminished since World War II, that it is virtually impossible to defeat this Russian undersea horde at sea using conventional warhead weapons. Obviously then, one would argue, the Russian use of their total submarine fleet would constitute a first rate threat to the United States, hence, as a counter-attack we would have to unleash the Strategic Air Command and any other weapon system capable of hitting the Russian mainland with atomic and hydrogen bombs. Therefore, one would question, why bother to develop techniques for defeating the Russian submarine at sea, since we can only hope to defeat this threat, by calling out the Sunday Punch team anyway?

The answer to this question is found in the statement that the hardware created by a nation will very likely somehow, somewhere be used. How that hardware will be used cannot be predicted. Thus, a world agreement against the use of atomic weapons could deter us from bringing a Sunday Punch to bear on the Russian bases, harbors, and supporting installations. One could argue, of course, that if the chips were down, we could use atomic weapons anyway. Perhaps so. But we, above all other countries, respect the opinion of the majority in our own nation; hence, we very likely will hold that same respect for the opinions on which a world agreement is based. So we could be faced with an antisubmarine war using conventional weapons.

Possibly, too, the Russians could sell or give a certain number of their ships to Communist bloc nations. The press is currently reporting the transfer of three Russian ships to Egypt. This number could be increased considerably and might apply to other nations, such as Communist China. Then in any limited action in which the United States might engage, perhaps as part of a United Nations force against either China, Egypt, or any Russian satellite nation, a reduced but important anti-submarine war could be waged at sea. How would this be fought in terms of atomic bombs on the Russian mainland?

Certainly these and other situations could occur. Hence, the mere fact that a potential enemy has certain hardware on hand is reason enough to develop various ways and means of combatting it under any and all circumstances. In fact, the mere existence of the Russian submarine fleet is in itself sufficient justification for making ASW one of the primary missions of the U.S. Navy.

As a matter of fact, the theory behind disarmament contains elements of this theme. If all nations agree not to build weapon systems, then obviously the hardware to create damage is not available when international tension arises; hence, idealistically, one can hope the matter in disagreement can be arbitrated before hardware can be built.

An interesting corollary to the certainty that created hardware will be used, and the uncertainty of how it will be used is this: The operational concepts which bring certain weapon systems into being may, in fact, never be valid when the hardware is finally used.

As an illustration, one sees the genesis in our own navy of the fleet submarine, which fought the Japanese Navy so successfully in World War II. This submarine was designed in the years before the war to have a high surface speed of twenty knots. To achieve this, it was given long, sleek hull lines, and a destroyer bow. The high surface speed was to allow it to operate with the fleet, hence it received its name, the "Fleet" submarine. However, when World War II arrived the designed high surface speed of this submarine was never used as called for in the fleet sub's original concept. Instead, the high surface speed was found extremely useful for the long transit from Pearl Harbor to the Japanese Empire waters, and for closing and attacking Japanese convoys on the surface at night.

As another example, one sees the present destroyer of all navies, which is now an antiaircraft, anti-submarine, shore bombardment, jack-of-all-trades. It came into being before World War I, under entirely different operational thinking. The destroyer was originally conceived as a high speed, highly maneuverable, gun-carrying ship to defend the fleet against the dagger thrust of motor-torpedo boats of equally high speed. Hence it received the name of "torpedo boat destroyer." Later the destroyer assumed the operational duties of the vehicle it replaced, and finally, when World War II arrived, it was considered ideal to carry the depth charges necessary to kill the Nazi U-boat.

In peacetime, who can tell exactly how in some future battle a weapon system will be used tactically? Many might guess at certain possibilities, but the only point which has any real certainty is this: Hardware once created will very likely be used!

Peacetime Tactical Development

The fourth and last thought which occurs from all the above discussion on tactical development is this. There are two definite reasons for tactical development in peacetime. Most obvious and first, tactics are developed in peacetime to produce procedures for using the hardware available. This creates the necessary degree of war readiness, now. The natural by-products of peacetime operating are lessons learned about the inadequacies of the available hardware. The destroyer skipper unable to attack his brother submarine skipper soon has facts to back a request for new and different weapons.

Second, and by far the most important reason, peacetime tactical development creates a corps of people who are trained mentally to solve tactical problems. Naturally one hopes to develop operational procedures of lasting validity, peace or war. But one element of wartime tactics will always be missing from even the most realistic of peacetime exercises. That element is the possible death or severe physical damage to those engaged. Furthermore, what the enemy will do, how he will operate, can only be determined in war, for, in fact, he himself is not quite exactly sure in peacetime. Hence, one strives in peacetime, not for complete and lasting tactical solutions, but only for the creation of a corps of courageous, willing, and thinking people who can solve these problems in war.

Conclusions

By way of conclusion, these points stand out. To view the effectiveness of a weapon system, one must think of a weapon-operation, that is, one must view, not only the hardware, but how the nation's commanding officer will use it. Tactics, then, can develop either through a weapon-system change or through a change in operational procedures. But leaders in wartime would do well not to count on a quick or miraculous improvement in the hardware of their weapon systems, when their country calls them forth to its defense. Rather they should count on a personal spirit, and mentality in themselves and their brothers-in-arms, developed through strenuous peacetime effort, which will permit them to do what they must with what they have. The fact that peacetime operational procedures must be thrown away is of no consequence. The fact that these leaders are flexible and alert enough to do so and can thereby achieve success is sufficient evidence that in peacetime they fulfilled their obligation to their country so as to be prepared for war.

People Count First

Properly, a postscript should be added to this paper to be sure its remarks are interpreted in the correct light. There is no denying that certain hardware, radar, the airplanes, and so forth, produced vast tactical changes in past wars. Certain new hardware produced in recent times, for example, the nuclear submarine, the guided missile, *etc.*, will continue this process of change, indeed, will accelerate it. But, unfortunately, it is virtually impossible to obtain exclusiveness of use on any weapon. Even now, the Press is reporting the building of nuclear submarines by the Russians. One continues to hope, of course, that one's industrial might will maintain a hardware lead, but even this is impossible when industrial giants face each other. As a matter of fact, one should seek after those hardware changes which will produce the quantum jumps in progress rather than squandering one's industrial effort on the changes which will produce only the marginal gains. But let no one forget that one and only one element will finally sway the balance, when a country must defend the things for which it stands. That element is people; people who believe, people who will act, people who can think, people who have what it takes to outfight the enemy.

4 "FROM 'FUTURISTIC WHIMSY' TO NAVAL REALITY"

Abraham Rabinovich

A scant six years after Soviet-built cruise missiles sank the Israeli destroyer *Eilat* in 1967, the Israeli navy was ready to fight and defeat Egyptian and Syrian missile ships with its own small missile ships. The little navy did not know when it might have to fight. It only knew its warships were obsolete, so it better prepare, and fast. Abraham Rabinovich relates the story of a swift recognition that navies were entering the missile age. This was followed by rapid negotiations for overseas construction and delivery of the first-generation Saar boats, which could carry Israeli-designed Gabriel missiles. But simultaneous with the procurement came the ugly recognition that the Israeli navy would have to defeat SS-N-2 Styx missiles that outranged its Gabriels.

Rabinovich shows how missile technology has to be accompanied by fleet combat doctrine, and new tactics practiced assiduously. Most battles between fleets in the missile era occurred during the 1973 Arab-Israeli War. The battles are the best laboratory we have for study of fleet-on-fleet combat and by which to measure offensive and defensive performance, because by far the most missiles were fired in anger then. The battles were also an illustration of a totally successful missile defense at sea: no casualties were suffered on the Israeli side, even though Syrian and Egyptian SS-N-2s outranged the Gabriels and were fired in big salvoes. The Israeli victories kept the sea lanes open for critical supplies to reach Israel during the intense fighting on the ground.

But the battles were fought over forty years ago, and much has changed. Indeed, more time has passed since those first *missile* salvoes were fired than in the thirty years that transpired between 1973 and 1943 when American destroyer attacks with *torpedo* salvoes were carried out perfectly in the Battle of Vella Gulf and the Battle of Cape Saint George in the Solomon Islands. In both instances the tacticians on the winning side recognized that exploitation of surprise was the key to victory. In both instances the winning side suffered no losses while nearly destroying an enemy that on paper was competitive or superior. In both instances the tactics of salvo warfare comprised a system of detection, deception, and timely weapon release that was executed by coordinated forces on the winning side. And in both instances the battles were fought at night. In 1973 an intense battle for air superiority was going on simultaneously, so no aircraft entered into the competition, a factor the Israeli navy anticipated and exploited. Now, forty years after the Arab-Israeli War, it is appropriate to say that combat in coastal waters will not be battles between two fleets, but land-sea fighting in which warships participate.

One should try for but not expect to achieve a loss-free victory. In July 2006, the Israeli navy lost a warship to a land-to-sea missile attack from Syria. Before we developed our winning torpedo salvo tactics in 1943, between August and December 1942 we were lucky when we could claim a draw against the more proficient Japanese navy in many night surface battles fought near Guadalcanal. It took us six months to abandon the obsolete column tactics with which we fought and frequently lost. A constant of naval tactics has been that the battles will be fast and furious, with good and bad surprises.

"FROM 'FUTURISTIC WHIMSY' TO NAVAL REALITY"

By Abraham Rabinovich, *Naval History* (June 2014): 41–47.

The Israeli navy's development of missile boats in the 1960s was an exceptional demonstration of national will—and the battles they fought in the Yom Kippur War were a turning point in naval warfare.

The officers converging on Israeli naval headquarters atop Haifa's Mount Carmel in late 1960 had been summoned to a brainstorming session by the navy's commander, Admiral Yohai Bin-Nun. There was only one item on the agenda: how to make a navy consisting of World War II castoffs, from aging destroyers to an icebreaker, relevant. The Defense Ministry had made clear that there was no money for new ships. The navy, it warned, might be downscaled to a coast guard if it could not reconstitute itself as a credible force within its limited budget.

From two days of discussion, an offbeat idea floated to the surface as if on its own accord. The government's weapons-development arm, Rafael, had produced a primitive guided missile, the Luz, which both the artillery corps and air force had rejected. If the Luz, with its 331-pound warhead, could be adapted to patrol boats, someone suggested, these cheap vessels would have the punch of cruisers. The suggestion was dismissed as futuristic whimsy by most of the participants. No missile boat existed in the West, but Admiral Bin-Nun assigned his deputy, Captain Shlomo Erell, to explore the idea.

Erell was the closest thing in the Israeli navy to a crusty professional sailor. Joining the British merchant marine in the Second World War, he participated in the Dunkirk evacuation and made the Murmansk and Atlantic convoy runs, surviving two torpedoings. The small-boat/big-punch concept intrigued him. In blissful ignorance of the difficulties that lay ahead, he formed a team to give shape to the boat circling at the center of his mind.

Laying the Foundation

Tested at sea, the Luz failed consistently. The missile was supposed to be brought onto target by an aimer with a joystick tracking a bright red flare on the Luz's tail through high-powered binoculars. But dense smoke caused by the humidity's effect on the missile's exhaust emissions at sea shrouded the flare.

An engineer at Rafael, Ori Even-Tov, had scorned the joystick approach from the start. It was, he argued, an attempt to fuse missile technology with a bow-and-arrow guidance system. Although Even-Tov had been at Rafael only a short time, he had earned a reputation as a brilliant engineer and a maverick difficult to control. His comments on the Luz gained no traction at Rafael, but at a demonstration of a new weapon in the Negev Desert, Even-Tov found himself sharing a tent with a naval officer. "I don't think the Luz is ever going to work as a sea-to-sea missile," Even-Tov told him. What it needed, he said, was an autonomous guidance system that would permit the missile itself to seek out the target. An altimeter would keep the missile at a fixed height above the water, and radar in the missile would guide it to target.

Even-Tov was born in Jerusalem and had not finished high school. Swept up in Israel's War of Independence in 1948, he served as a platoon commander and stayed on in the army. At age 25 he traveled to the United States where he graduated from Columbia University, obtained an engineering degree at Drexel, and served as a project manager at a large defense plant before returning to Israel. As he had hoped, his remarks to the naval officer reached Erell, who consulted with managers at Israel Aircraft Industries (IAI), Rafael's main rival.

Israel's fledgling military industries had funding and were eager for projects to sink their teeth into. "The IAI's a good horse to run with," Erell told Bin-Nun. Even-Tov was contacted by IAI and agreed to jump ship. Settling into his office in the firm's headquarters in Lod, he asked for a mathematician to work with him and a set of American textbooks on airborne radar and allied fields. Guided missiles existed in the West, but Israel was not privy to their secrets. However, textbook theory was available, which Even-Tov and his assistant proceeded to digest.

The navy was stunned in 1962 when it learned that the Soviets had built their own missile boats and were providing them to Egypt and Syria. Admiral Bin-Nun requested an urgent meeting with Deputy Defense Minister Shimon Peres (who today, at 90, is Israel's president). Bin-Nun warned that the refitted

Arab fleets could strangle Israel's maritime lifeline. If Israel acquired half a dozen missile boats, he said, it could deal with the threat. An appropriate boat platform had been identified. Two of his officers touring foreign navies had gone to sea on board a German Jaguar torpedo boat. The Jaguar had begun life in the Second World War as a Schnellboot (S-boat) harassing Allied shipping. The vessel impressed the officers with its power and ease of handling. Although not very comfortable for the crew, it had ample room for armaments and electronic apparatus. "This is a ship of war," the officers reported.

What was needed now, Bin-Nun said, was funding. "You have my blessings and you'll get the money," Peres assured him.

Five years before, Peres had driven through a snowstorm to the Bavarian hometown of Germany's defense minister, Franz-Josef Strauss. Israeli Prime Minister David Ben-Gurion had decided that Israel's security situation obliged it to seek help from the country that had murdered six million Jews little more than a decade before. During a five-hour talk, Peres spelled out to Strauss Israel's need for military equipment. The subsequent German defense budget would include an allocation of $60 million over five years for "aid in the form of equipment." The beneficiary was not mentioned but the equipment list would now include six Jaguar torpedo boats.

"Minor" Modifications

Captain Erell had larceny in his heart when he flew to Germany in March 1963. At his meeting with defense officials in Bonn, he said that the Jaguars destined for Israel required modifications. After listening to Erell spell out the modifications at length, the head of the German team leaned forward and said bemusedly: "Ja, ja, very interesting captain. But tell me, don't you want a grand piano on this boat, too?"

What Erell wanted was a new boat. He requested permission to meet with the Jaguar's builders, the Bremen firm of Lurssen Brothers. Here he found immediate understanding. Israeli naval architect Commander Haim Shahal, who accompanied him, told the shipbuilders that the Jaguar was too small to contain all the systems planned for it. Would it be possible to insert two more of the frames that formed its hull to stretch the vessel by 7 feet 10 inches, giving it a total length of 147 feet 8 inches? He also wanted to repartition the internal space. Lurssen's chief naval architect, Herr Waldemuth, grasped what the Israelis were getting at. Making his own calculations, he said, "We can do it."

Growing Pains

The first test of Even-Tov's radical redesign of the Luz came in 1964, and was witnessed by members of the General Staff, top defense officials, and observers from Rafael. The first missile arced into the sky and plummeted straight down. So did the next two. Raucous hoots came from the Rafael delegation. The next test, three months later, was a duplicate of the first. "Ori, we'd also like to see it work occasionally," a senior official said tartly. This time, Even-Tov asked for nine months to prepare for the next test.

Back in the IAI plant the next day, Even-Tov reckoned that the project was unlikely to survive another failure. A technician asking to speak with him interrupted his cogitations. The man, Yaacov Becker, had only recently joined the team, which was top-heavy with engineers and scientists. Becker believed the problem was that the altimeter packaging was not robust enough to withstand the launch. Although Becker had only a vocational school education, Even-Tov had already marked him as a craftsman.

"Do you have any proposals?" Even-Tov asked.

"Give me a few days."

When Becker submitted his plan, Even-Tov summoned the two senior engineers dealing with the altimeter. Both termed the plan unworkable, adding that they would rather resign than pursue it. "In that case," said Even-Tov, "your resignations are accepted as of now." He appointed Becker in their place, with 30 men working under him.

The third test of the missile, in 1965, was on a secluded stretch of coast south of Haifa. The Luz had acquired a new name—the Gabriel—but it had yet to prove it could fly. The observers on the dunes looked funereal as the countdown began over loudspeakers: "Three, two, one, launch." The missile arced into the sky and fell like a stone. There was hardly time for despair to set in before the second missile was launched. Reaching the top of its trajectory it seemed to hang in midair. It was several seconds before Even-Tov realized that the missile was not defying gravity but was leveling off and heading out to sea. The crowd cheered. It cheered again when the third missile struck the target. Even-Tov turned to look at the dune where the Rafael observers had been standing, but they were gone.

The missile-boat project now had momentum, but a new set of problems suddenly descended—political. The Arab states had learned of the arms deal and threatened to break diplomatic relations with Bonn. Embarrassed, Germany told Israel it would give it the money to have the boats built elsewhere. Erell balked. Israel, he insisted, also needed the revised Jaguar plans and the license to use them. Germany said it couldn't do that for fear of Arab ire. An aide called Erell's attention to an article in *Jane's*, the British defense publication, mentioning that Lurssen was cooperating with a shipbuilding firm in Cherbourg in building patrol boats. When contacted, the French firm said it would be able to have the plans and license for the modified Jaguar transferred to it. And so it was.

Construction of the first missile boat at the Cherbourg shipyard, Les Constructions Mecaniques de Normandie, began in 1965. An Israeli naval contingent took up residence in the town to test the boats—dubbed the Saar (Storm) class—as they came off the ways, ostensibly as patrol boats. Not until they arrived in Israel would they be fitted out as missile boats. The first vessel was subject to 10,000 miles of punishing sea tests, sometimes running down the Normandy coast past the D-Day beaches.

Erell, who had succeeded Bin-Nun as navy commander, persuaded the General Staff to double the number of missile boats to 12 to enable the navy to cope simultaneously with the Egyptian and Syrian fronts. Meanwhile, at naval headquarters, a planning team was translating the grand vision into tangible dimensions. The team, which would eventually number several hundred men, was broken into subgroups charged with specific aspects. How many masts were needed to accommodate the dense electronic array? What procedures would enable seamen in battle—not just engineers in laboratory conditions—to fire the missile effectively? What to do about mutual interferences—electronic, noise, electromagnetic—among systems located near one another? The questions were endless and each answer carried with it new problems.

Israel's military industries, reaching into new areas of technology, were able to provide many solutions. However, key elements like fire-control systems, which aim the guns and missiles, had to be developed at firms abroad. The young Israeli naval engineers sent to oversee this work gradually overcame their diffidence vis-à-vis the veteran continental engineers.

Team leaders in Haifa met regularly to report to each other on progress and thrash out differences. Search radar, which scanned for enemy ships, and fire-control radar, which guided the missiles onto target, vied with each other for higher position on the mast; guns and torpedo tubes elbowed each other for choice position on the deck; sonar argued against being thrown overboard to save weight. The flow of information was constant, and the pace manic. Tests were constantly being set, reports presented, contracts for components signed. The intensity would last for years, laced for all with moments of despair, when it seemed mad to have attempted the enterprise. Looking about him, Erell was convinced that no major power had ever put as much energy into the design of a battleship.

A New Threat

For most of the men involved, this would be the greatest adventure of their lives. A country of three million inhabitants with no sophisticated industrial base had taken upon itself to develop a major weapon system. Officers who had sailed in nothing but hand-me-downs found themselves plunging through uncharted waters at the frontier of military science. It was an exhilarating experience, edged by the knowledge that war was waiting in the wings.

It came before they were ready, in June 1967. It ended after six days with an astonishing Israeli victory. The navy had taken almost no part. Three months later, however, the destroyer *Eilat*, flagship of the fleet, was patrolling off Sinai when lookouts saw a flaring of light off Port Said, 14 miles west. A minute later, a Styx missile exploded in the heart of the ship. Three more missiles would hit, sending the *Eilat* to the bottom. Of the 200-man crew, 47 were killed and 91 wounded.

The West had known of the existence of the Styx but not its precision or power. A small boat on the horizon had sunk a warship ten times its size. The world's navies would have to adjust to a new reality. Israel's was the only one already doing so, but it now had a major correction to make. Intelligence had learned that the range of the Styx was 27 miles, more than twice the Gabriel's 12 miles. The Saars would have to cross a 15-mile "missile belt" in which they would be vulnerable to the Styx without being able to respond. Erell asked his chief electronics officer, Captain Herut Tsemach, what could be done. Guessing at the parameters of the radar his counterpart in Leningrad had installed in the Styx, Tsemach devised electronic countermeasures. Whether they worked would have to await the test of battle.

In Cherbourg, boats were launched every two or three months and sailed to Israel after their sea tests. This routine changed with the launching of Boat Seven. The head of the Israeli military purchasing-mission in Paris, retired Admiral Mordecai Limon, learned that the French were about to impose an embargo on the boats for political reasons, even though Israel had already paid for them. Limon telephoned the commander of the Israeli contingent in Cherbourg and suggested elliptically that Boat Six, which had just completed her sea tests, and Boat Seven, which had not yet started them, make a run for it without informing the French naval authorities. The boats succeeded in getting away. A few days later, France imposed the embargo.

The Ruse

The embargo did not affect construction of the remaining boats, only their departure. Limon urged Jerusalem to permit the remaining five boats to escape after the last was completed. Unwilling to risk diplomatic rupture with France, the government authorized the boats' departure only if it could be done "not illegally." As the last boat neared completion in December 1969, Limon resorted to a sleight of hand. He waived Israel's claim on the boats, and a Norwegian shipowner—a friend of a friend of Limon—offered to buy them, ostensibly to supply offshore oil rigs in the North Sea. French customs authorities granted permission for the boats to depart. Fearing that this legal fiction was too thin to pass close scrutiny, Limon advised the commander of the Cherbourg contingent, Captain Israel Kimche, to get away as quickly and quietly as possible.

The Israeli Defense Ministry, rising to the occasion, organized a quasi-military operation, fitting out a freighter and a car ferry with extra fuel tanks and pumping equipment to refuel the boats at sea since the fleeing vessels would not be able to enter ports for fear of seizure. Israeli freighters, diverted from their regular runs, were spaced along the 3,200-mile escape route in case the boats encountered trouble. Scores of Israeli naval crewmen in civilian dress were given passports and flown to Paris. In small groups they made their way by train to Cherbourg, where they were hidden in the boats below decks.

Departure was set for early Christmas Eve, but a force 9 gale kept even large freighters from venturing out. At 0200, when the wind began to shift, Captain Kimche cast off. Battered as they crossed the roiling Bay of Biscay, the boats reached the Portuguese cove where the first refueling vessel was waiting for them. (The other was off Lampedusa, the southernmost island of Italy.)

When the French discovered the ruse the infuriated defense minister proposed that the air force interdict the vessels, but calmer voices prevailed. The international press leaped on the caper with glee. Television crews rented planes to search for the boats—some over the North Sea route to Norway, some over the Mediterranean. A press plane finally sighted five small boats racing along the coast of North Africa, as far from French waters as possible. On New Year's Eve 1970, the boats anchored in Haifa.

The next three years and nine months were spent converting the Saars into missile boats, developing tactics for a totally new type of warfare, and training crews. It was not until the first week of October 1973 that all the boats joined in a flotilla maneuver. The day after they returned to base the Yom Kippur War broke out.

The First At-Sea Missile Battles

The flotilla commander, Commander Michael Barkai, immediately dispatched a half dozen boats south to block any Egyptian sally. With nightfall, he led five others north into Syrian waters. From the radio in his boat's combat information center (CIC), the feisty officer addressed the other captains. Their objective, he said, was to draw the Syrian missile boats out of Latakia, Syria's main harbor, and sink them. "If they don't come out, I mean to sail in and destroy them with guns. We're going to go in close enough to heave our docking lines if we have to."

Eighteen miles southwest of Latakia, the task force disabled with gunfire a Syrian patrol boat on picket duty. Barkai left a boat behind to finish her off. Within minutes, the lead vessel picked up a minesweeper 15 miles away racing for Latakia. The overeager captain fired when he reached maximum Gabriel range. Barkai groaned. In the two minutes the missile was in the air, the fleeing target pulled out of range.

On board another Saar, the *Reshef*, Captain Micha Ram waited until he was 11 miles from target. Personally verifying that the radar was locked onto the correct target and that it was in adequate range, he pressed a white button labeled "permission to fire." Two minutes later, cheers were heard from the bridge as a flaring on the horizon signaled a hit.

Almost simultaneously, search radar picked up three vessels close to shore. The Syrian missile boats were coming out. On the bridge, balls of light could be seen arcing over the horizon. In the CIC below, fast-moving dots appeared on radar screens. The first missile battle at sea had begun. The boats' loudspeakers erupted with the warning, "missiles, missiles, missiles." The boats activated electronic deceptors and jammers, which analyzed the characteristics of the Styx's radar and sent back signals on the same wavelength to create false targets. At the same time, the boats zigzagged wildly and sent up rockets that released chaff—aluminum strips intended to further confuse the Styx's radar.

The navy's war room in Israel heard the missile warning. Then the radio went silent. Herut Tsemach, who had retired from the navy, was back for the war. The lives of the 200 men in the task force depended on the accuracy of his educated guess about the Styx's capabilities. After two minutes, Barkai's voice broke the silence. "Missiles in the water." The normally reserved Tsemach let out an Indian whoop as cheering filled the room. Cupping the top of his head with one hand, Tsemach spun himself around the room as if he were a top.

Raising their electronic umbrellas, the Saars charged across the missile belt at 40 knots. One of the Syrian boats came directly at them. Lieutenant

Commander Arye Shefler commanded the Israeli boat now in the lead, the *Gaash*. The Syrian boat fired first, at half her maximum range. The Styx was still in the air when the *Gaash* reached Gabriel range. Shefler pressed the "permission to fire" button. As the Gabriel launched, the Styx exploded in the water, but the *Gaash*'s electronic sensors detected another Styx lifting off. The first Gabriel was still in the air when Shefler launched another. Theoretically, the dueling missile boats could have blown each other simultaneously out of the water, but the second Styx exploded harmlessly before the first Gabriel had completed its trajectory. Meanwhile, the *Miznak*, Barkai's command vessel, had fired a Gabriel at a second Syrian boat. The men watching from the bridges of the Israeli vessels saw the horizon torn by jagged light. Across the water came the roll of two explosions, a few seconds apart.

Barkai, who was watching the battle on the radar screen in the CIC below deck called to his operations officer, "Where are the Syrian boats?"

"Sunk."

Barkai was stunned. He had sunk enemy vessels innumerable times during exercises on a simulator, but it hadn't occurred to him that they would disappear from the screen the same way in reality. There was one more Syrian boat to account for, and radar showed her heading for shore. With no more missiles, her commander ran his boat onto the beach, and the crew clambered off. Despite fire from shore batteries, Barkai went in close and destroyed her with gunfire.

It was light when the returning Saars approached Haifa. Word of their stunning success had spread through the city and the breakwater was lined with spectators. Barkai decided not to tie brooms to the mast in the traditional symbol of a clean sweep. The boats had left a lot of Syrian sailors at the bottom of the sea, he said. Any flaunting "wouldn't be respectful to them or ourselves."

On to Egypt

Two nights later, it was Egypt's turn as three pairs of Saars moved west toward Alexandria. Sensors picked up indications of four missile boats emerging from the harbor and moving east. Off Baltim, near where Nelson had sunk Napoleon's fleet, the signals grew stronger. As they closed range, crewmen at the CIC consoles and screens began shouting: "Here they come. Four of them. Right at us."

The sensors indicated an Egyptian missile launch at maximum Styx range. Despite Barkai's cool demeanor, he felt fear at every salvo. The Saars' antimissile devices created many diversionary targets, but the boats themselves were also targets. The Styxes exploded in the sea, their half-ton charges sending up geysers. The Egyptians kept coming, firing two more salvos in the next ten minutes. At 18 miles distance, they turned back. The pursuit was on.

"We're going to close to ten miles before firing," Barkai said to his captains. "Anybody who fires longer I will dismiss on the spot." He divided the targets among his commanders. After 25 minutes, a boat on the northern wing reported herself within range. She fired and hit. An Egyptian boat in the center was hit moments later. A third, running close to the shore, was hit by a Gabriel but did not sink, having settled on a sandbank. The fourth Egyptian boat escaped back to Alexandria when the Israeli vessel pursuing her developed engine trouble.

The Arab missile boats did not venture out to sea again, limiting themselves to sniping from heir harbor mouths. The Soviet-made boats had no electronic defenses and were sitting ducks once the Israelis were able to thwart the Styx. Israel's quick victory at sea enabled more than 100 freighters to reach Haifa with much needed supplies during the three-week war. There were no Israeli casualties. Naval warfare had a new face.

The Saars continued to attack Syrian ports almost every night and destroy oil tank farms along the coast. They dueled with Syrian boats firing from behind foreign freighters in their harbors. Gabriels inadvertently sank three such freighters, one of them Russian.

Shlomo Erell, who had made it all happen, joined the flotilla during one of its final sorties. The retired admiral was captivated by the way Barkai and his captains—one of whom was Erell's son, Udi—coordinated their movements as the boats slalomed between plumes thrown up by missiles and shore batteries. From the port of Tartus, he saw four Styxes appear in the sky like a formation of planes. The bright lights looked as if they were heading straight for his boat. Erell was petrified, but if the others on the bridge were they didn't show it. "They're beginning to turn," the bridge officer said. To Erell, they still seemed heading straight between his eyes but after a few seconds he could see them beginning to succumb to the tug of the phantom decoys.

The complex systems crammed into the small boats had passed the ultimate test better than he could have imagined. Recalling his meeting in the German defense ministry ten years before, Erell smiled to himself and thought, "They've even put in the grand piano."

This article is adapted from the author's eBook *The Boats of Cherbourg: The Navy That Stole Its Own Boats and Revolutionized Naval Warfare*, which is a revised and expanded version of his previous work *The Boats of Cherbourg: The Secret Israeli Operation That Revolutionized Naval Warfare* (Naval Institute Press, 1988). The books are based primarily on more than 100 interviews conducted by the author. He can be reached at abra@netvision.net.il. Additional sources of information for this article include:

LTGEN Fouad Abu Zikra, Egyptian Navy, "The Role of the Naval Forces in the War of October, 1973." Paper delivered at international symposium, Cairo, October 1975.

RADM Zeev Almog, Israeli Navy, "Israel's Naval Theatre," *Israel Defense Forces Journal*, Spring 1986.

Herbert Coleman, "Gabriel Outmatches Soviet Styx," *Aviation Week*, 10 December 1973.

RADM Erell Shlomo, Israeli Navy, "Israel Saar FPBs Pass Combat Test in Yom Kippur War," U.S. Naval Institute *Proceedings*, September 1974.

CAPT Peleg Lapid, Israeli Navy, Ret., "Electronics in the Israeli Navy," *Israel Defense Forces Journal*, December 1984.

"Mideast War Spurs Missile R&D Effort," *Aviation Week*, 31 December 1973.

RADM Binyamin Rahav, Israeli Navy, "Strategic and Naval Policy," *Jerusalem Post*, 19 October 1987.

5 "WILLIAM B. CUSHING"

LCDR Thomas J. Cutler, USN (Ret.)

Lieutenant William B. Cushing, USN, was an exemplar of a daring officer who fought single-ship actions superbly. I have chosen the most famous example of Cushing's exploits in the Civil War to illustrate how single-ship tactics are different from fleet tactics. He succeeded in part because in a duel, no cooperation with other units is necessary.

Lieutenant Thomas Cochrane's achievements exceed even those of Cushing, with bold successes at sea and on land in the Napoleonic Wars. I recommend reading Donald Thomas' book, *Cochrane: Britannia's Sea Wolf*, published in the Naval Institute Press' Bluejacket series, not for its tactical lessons but for the sheer pleasure of reading about his exploits and learning the personality of the young officer who was the model for Jack Aubrey's sea-going adventures in Patrick O'Brian's *Master and Commander* and *Post Captain*.

Today we call single-ship skills "Tactics, Techniques, and Procedures," but Cushing and Cochrane show that something more is required to defeat bigger ships. Both young officers achieved victories with peerless courage, imagination, and quick decision-making in a crisis.

More recent examples of a combat duel's uniqueness are found in air-to-air combat, exemplified by Gregory "Pappy" Boyington, Butch

O'Hare, and Jimmy Thach of "Thach Weave" fame. The same uniqueness is true of skillful submarine tacticians like Gene Fluckey, Dudley "Mush" Morten, and Dick O'Kane.

The sinking of the CSS *Albemarle* brought Cushing to the attention of the flag officers charged with blockading the Confederacy's Atlantic Coast. He was repeatedly employed, rising to the rank of commander by the end of the war. After the war when Commander Cushing commanded the USS *Wyoming*, he was drawn into the middle of "the *Virginius* Affair" in 1874 at Santiago, Cuba. As usual, he exhibited forthrightness and courage, in what was going to be a precursor cause of the Spanish-American War. More to our purpose in this anthology, *Wyoming* also participated that same year in the first attempts after the Civil War to exercise our Atlantic warships as a battle fleet, anticipating the frustrations and triumphs described in the next chapter, taken from Commander James Rentfrow's 2014 book, *Home Squadron.*

Considering the importance and frequency of duels of all descriptions, it is curious that I could find no essay on the *tactics* of one-on-one combat. Nevertheless, there is an extensive literature describing where the combat advantages lay, most famously by Frederick W. Lanchester in his *Aircraft in Warfare* (1915). In fleet actions, numbers of well-manned ships matter most when the tactics and training are sound. In a series of single-unit actions like Lieutenant Cushing's, individual prowess and combat experience matter most. But Lanchester was not the first to describe the special advantage of numbers in fleet actions. You will find in the essay by Bradley Fiske, written ten years before Lanchester, a quantitative description of the "Lanchester square law" phenomenon.

Tom Cutler is on the staff of the Naval Institute Press, where he has written and published several books. His narrative of William Barker Cushing's best-remembered exploit is taken from his Naval Institute *Proceedings* series, "Lest We Forget."

"WILLIAM B. CUSHING"

By LCDR Thomas Cutler, USN (Ret.), U.S. Naval Institute *Proceedings* (October 2003): 126.

The Confederate ironclad *Albemarle* was 122-feet long, built of solid ten-inch thick Southern pine encased in railroad-track armor four-inches thick, and was armed with two 100-pound rifled guns mounted on both sides that gave them a clear shot in almost any direction. The presence of this behemoth in the Roanoke River posed a serious danger to Union forces, threatening the blockading forces in the area and preventing any Union advances down the Carolina coast.

Ignoring the obvious danger of such a reckless mission, Lieutenant William B. Cushing and 13 other sailors crammed into a small launch armed with a single spar torpedo and headed upriver on a dark, drizzling night to take on the iron monster in her lair. For eight miles, the little launch made its way past enemy guard posts on shore and picket boats in the river.

At about 0300, Cushing saw a large black silhouette looming out of the darkness. As he maneuvered closer, sentries on the *Albemarle* spotted the craft and sounded the alarm. Cushing charged at the ironclad at full speed. Bullets whipped and cracked all about the men in the launch, several passing through Cushing's clothing, as they continued to close.

The defenders had rigged a floating fence of chained logs around the *Albemarle* to protect her from exactly what Cushing had in mind. Surmising that the logs had been in the water for quite some time and probably were slippery, Cushing plunged ahead, driving the launch right onto the logs.

Perched there, the Union sailors were staring point blank into the muzzle of one of the *Albemarle*'s big guns as her crew frantically loaded the weapon. Undaunted by the harrowing sight, Cushing lowered the boom and drove the torpedo into the side of the ship, just below the waterline. Union torpedo and Confederate gun went off nearly simultaneously.

Miraculously, Cushing and another sailor survived, escaping into the river. The other men perished or were captured. But the ironclad *Albemarle* sank to the bottom of the river, never to rise again. On hearing of this daring exploit, Secretary of the Navy Gideon Welles called William Cushing "the hero of the war." Since that October night in 1864, five ships have been named USS *Cushing* (TB-1, DD-55, DD-376, DD-797, and DD-985).

6 "TOWARD A NEW IDENTITY, 1882–1888"

(Selections from chapter 2 of *Home Squadron*)

James C. Rentfrow

The next two vignettes, written more than a century apart, form a couplet describing how tactical innovation and technological innovation must proceed hand in hand. Both examples emphasize fleet operations and what the best U.S. Navy leaders thought it took for ships in formation to become proficient in a sea battle. Both describe leaders, among them Stephen B. Luce, who emphasized fleet evolutions at sea for combat readiness.

Commander Rentfrow is a former EA-6B flight officer who now teaches naval history at the U.S. Naval Academy. His book describes the difficulty of improving fleet tactics in a Navy that was accustomed to being an arm of the State Department, on call to "show the flag" while operating as single ships or in small detachments. The progress achieved by exercising as a fleet was just good enough to defeat the second-rate Spanish fleet and put American forces safely ashore for expeditionary operations in Cuba and, though not Rentfrow's subject, also in the Philippines.

It is well known that when Alfred T. Mahan was brought by Luce to the newly founded Naval War College, the theory of sea power

Mahan espoused in his first classic, *The Influence of Sea Power upon History, 1660–1783,* emphasized command of the sea achieved by capital ships that defeated enemy capital ships in decisive battles. Perhaps, just perhaps, Mahan and Luce were doing some needed marketing of steel-hulled warships for the New Navy and their role in big fleet battles. As the battleship era emerged soon thereafter, Mahan could point to *war-winning* sea battles, two in the Sino-Japanese War in 1894, two in the Spanish-American War in 1898, and two in the Russo-Japanese War in 1905. But when, under Teddy Roosevelt and other advocates of a strong Navy, our battleships were being built, Mahan's later writings and those of Sir Julian Corbett would broaden the lens of sea power's influence and play down decisive battles as *sufficient* for a Navy that must also keep the sea lanes open and project power ashore.

Home Squadron foreshadows how a Navy that began from humble roots and wooden ships in 1874 would soon become a major sea power with battleships as the backbone of the fighting fleet. Rentfrow shows that the tactical operations at sea were often inspired by Admiral Luce. Despite Luce's reputation for establishing the Naval War College to study policy and strategy, his objective was coequally to develop tactics and improve the technologies of the fleet. We will see the same objective in the example from Bradley Fiske, which follows. The wisdom of Luce and Fiske is particularly worth reflection now, because of what it took to overcome traditionalists and rebuild the Navy as a twentieth-century fighting fleet, just before a century of peace at sea under the Pax Britannica came to an end with the rise of Imperial Germany. There are both similarities and differences with the situation today, as the U.S. Navy adjusts from skills of projecting power from the sea to restoring the skills of fighting a fleet and employing submarines to sink enemy surface ships once again.

"TOWARD A NEW IDENTITY, 1882–1888"

(Selections from chapter 2 of *Home Squadron: The U.S. Navy on the North Atlantic Station*) by James C. Rentfrow (Naval Institute Press, 2014): 50–53, 60–63.

Rear Admiral Luce and the Naval War College

One officer who was determined to push for a more systematic approach to fleet training and readiness for combat was then-Commo. Stephen B. Luce. Luce was the epitome of that rare breed of officer who was both exceptionally successful at sea and a pathbreaking leader ashore. He, perhaps more than any naval officer of the nineteenth century, understood that a "fleet" was more than just a collection of ships. He both articulated and then put into action a comprehensive system of education. In 1841, as a fourteen-year-old, he signed on board the USS *Congress* as a midshipman and moved through the ranks over the next twenty years. After distinguished service during the Civil War, Luce's association with the North Atlantic Squadron began with his tour of duty as the commanding officer of Rear Admiral LeRoy's flagship, *Hartford,* from 1 November 1875 to 21 August 1877. Although he was not present during the Key West exercises of 1874, we know that he understood the importance of that initial set of maneuvers, since his personal papers contain a full set of copies of all the reports submitted by Rear Admiral Case. Luce would, however, have been present for the landing exercises held in 1876. As the commanding officer of the flagship, he would have been privy to Rear Admiral LeRoy's frustration that year as planned fleet tactical exercises off Port Royal were rendered impossible to carry out by Navy Department tasking, which scattered his warships throughout the North Atlantic Squadron's operating area. It was a pattern that would repeat itself during Luce's career with the North Atlantic Squadron: high hopes of executing fleet training undermined by other duties. After leaving command of *Hartford,* Luce turned to naval education and training. He successfully established the New York State Maritime School, then spent the years 1877–83 in various positions associated with training naval apprentices, including command of the U.S. Training Ship *Minnesota* and command of the Apprentice Training Squadron.

His interests extended to education for officers as well, which led to his most lasting contribution as the founder and first president of the Naval War College at Newport, Rhode Island. In *Professors of War*, Ronald Spector argues that the foundation of the NWC was an important step in the professionalization of the naval officer corps. The opportunity for postgraduate professional interaction, when added to the initial bonding experience at the Naval Academy, the work of the Naval Institute at Annapolis, and the networking influence of various military-themed periodicals, was a major move for the profession. As such, the foundation of the NWC is a subject that has received its share of attention from naval historians. Typically the narrative focuses on the study of strategy and the cast of characters usually features Alfred Thayer Mahan and his ideas about the political-economic role of a navy in the shaping of national destiny. While correct, this interpretation does not give enough attention to Luce's belief in the importance of development of operational naval tactics in his fight to establish the Naval War College. Luce had a passion for putting naval theory into practice. He was fundamentally interested in the daily work associated with operating large ships together. One of the reasons that Luce felt that something like a war college was necessary was that the new naval professional of the 1880s would have to learn to fight entire squadrons of ships together as a unit.

After much lobbying, on 3 May 1884, Luce was ordered, along with Cdr. William T. Sampson and Cdr. C. F. Goodrich, to "consider and report upon the whole subject of a post graduate school or school of application, to be established by the Navy Department for officers of the Navy." The report that these three officers submitted the following year specifically noted, under the heading "PRACTICAL EXERCISES," "The North Atlantic Squadron affords the nearest approach to be found to a proper course in naval tactics. It should be assembled once a year, and during a stated period, go through a series of fleet evolutions, gunnery practice with the latest types of ordnance, the landing of seamen for military operations, boat operations, torpedo attack and defense, etc., having the class on board for instruction." It is evident that from the beginning, the Naval War College was not intended by Luce to be simply a classroom-based institution.

Before it had even been officially chartered, the NWC concept included the study and development of formation steaming tactics, with the North Atlantic Squadron acting as the laboratory.

On 26 July 1884, Commodore Luce was ordered to take command of the North Atlantic Squadron. It was to be a temporary position, as Luce had already been tapped to open the new Naval War College later that year, but he was determined to make the most of his brief opportunity to command ships at sea. On 10 July 1884, *Tennessee*, *Vandalia*, *Alliance*, and *Yantic* got under way from the squadron anchorage off Staten Island and headed for Portsmouth, New Hampshire, where the change of command was to take place. Rear Admiral Cooper took advantage of having four ships steaming together to carry out one final set of fleet exercises under his flag. Moving out of New York Harbor in column, the ships commenced exercises at 9:10 a.m. Nine more days of exercises followed, until the squadron arrived at Portsmouth, New Hampshire, where they met *Swatara*. After conducting the change of command, the five ships of the North Atlantic Squadron, together with the ships of the Training Squadron, participated in the reception for the Greely Relief Expedition.

From Portsmouth, *Tennessee*, *Vandalia*, *Swatara*, *Yantic*, and *Alliance* got under way on 6 August and conducted ten days of tactical exercises, including a landing of the naval brigade on Gardiner's Island on 11–13 August. From the ships of the squadron, 660 men were landed under the command of *Tennessee*'s commanding officer, Capt. J. N. Miller. Luce proudly noted that it had been a surprise exercise, with the landing orders given after the squadron had left Portsmouth for Newport, and that it was the largest exercise of its kind ever conducted on as little notice. The squadron arrived in Newport on 16 August. Once in Narragansett Bay, Luce had the ships of his squadron conduct measured mile speed and tactical diameter tests. Knowing exactly how many revolutions needed to be ordered for each ship to make a given speed, as well as knowing the arc each ship would scribe through the water at a given rudder angle, was crucial to the ability of a squadron to operate together and was information that was typically lacking at this formative stage. Officers of the deck were previously expected to carry out tactical maneuvers by "seaman's eye" rather than rely on data. In the days before instrumentation, maneuvers were made much more difficult without a reliable way to know how fast each ship was going. By immediately ordering speed trials for his new command, Luce showed that he recognized this fact and he intended his squadron to spend a lot of time operating together. Even before the official opening of the Naval War College, Luce was doing his best to fulfill his vision of the North Atlantic Squadron as a squadron of evolution, working out tactical problems studied at the NWC through actual exercises at sea. In fact, the board's selection of Newport, Rhode Island, as the permanent location for the college had a lot to do with the fact that the proximity of the deep water of the Narragansett Bay made it easy for the entire North Atlantic Squadron to call at Newport and coordinate fleet exercises with the college. However, Luce's first tour as commander in chief of the North Atlantic Squadron was short lived, as Congress approved the secretary of the navy's recommendation to open the Naval War College based on the report of Luce's board. Naturally, he was tapped to be the first president of the college, which cut short—for the moment—his squadron command tour. In fact, much of Luce's correspondence during this period was focused more on his work to get the college up and operating than it was on his position as a squadron commander in chief. On 20 September 1884, on board *Tennessee* anchored in Newport Harbor, Luce turned over command of the North Atlantic Squadron to Rear Adm. James E. Jouett. He then went ashore to take possession of the abandoned poorhouse on Coasters Harbor Island and begin the work of establishing the Naval War College. . . .

From New York, Luce corresponded with General Sheridan of the Army, suggesting that the Marines participate in joint Army-Navy exercises in 1888. He also carried on a regular dialogue with Commodore Walker and the secretary of the navy about available ships and their possible ports of call for the next summer. The initial plan was for Luce to take his warships, in company, on a tour of the southern ports, namely, New Orleans, Mobile, Pensacola, Savannah, and Charleston, then proceed north. It made sense, the squadron having spent the last two summers visiting northern ports. It appeared that Luce would have *Richmond* (his flagship), *Atlanta* (the first of the New Steel Navy cruisers), *Yantic*,

Dolphin, and *Galena.* This was not a large squadron, but there were enough ships to work through some tactical problems and train the officers of the squadron in handling their ships in formation.

The first indication that Luce was not going to be able to carry out his planned exercises in the summer was a request for support from the U.S. minister at San Domingo. On 11 January 1888, only ten days after Walker had expressed the approval of the Navy Department for Luce's training plan, Walker wrote Luce a somewhat apologetic letter in which he instructed him to detach a ship to serve the needs of the State Department. In July Luce's flagship *Richmond* was summoned for service on the Asiatic station. He was given *Pensacola* as a replacement, but she was unseaworthy, so he would be forced to transfer his flag to another, smaller, ship if he wanted to lead at sea. Meanwhile, political conditions in Haiti were deteriorating throughout the summer, culminating in an order from the Navy Department in August to send a ship to Port-au-Prince.

About this time, a letter arrived from the Navy Department asking Luce's opinion on summer training plans for his squadron. It should have been obvious at this point to anyone bothering to pay attention in the Navy Department that Luce had at his command only two ships. Training of any sort, other than perhaps to send signals to one another, was completely out of the question. The letter was the last straw. On 28 July 1888, Luce fired off a seven-page reply from New York in which he described his attempt to put together a coherent training plan for that summer. He detailed the detachment of his ships, one by one, for tasking to support the State Department, and he questioned, with astonishment, the attempt by the Navy Department to charge the War Department for any coal expended carrying soldiers in Navy ships during combined exercises. He lamented his inability to carry out his vision of making the North Atlantic Squadron a "school of practical instruction" that would exercise the theoretical concepts developed by the Naval War College:

> The *fundamental idea* [emphasis added] is to make theoretical instruction and practical exercise go hand in hand; or, in other words, to correlate the work of the Squadron and that of the College. In the lecture

room certain tactical propositions are laid down, or war problems given out, to the officers under instruction. Their merit is then tested in the School of Application, the Squadron, and the result afterwards discussed in the lecture room. This system raises our Squadron exercises to a higher plane than those of any other known to me, and places our Navy, comparatively insignificant in all else, in advance of the Navies of the world in respect to professional education.

The 28 July 1888 letter from Luce to Secretary of the Navy Whitney is a pivotal piece of Luce's correspondence, second only perhaps to the letter inviting Alfred Thayer Mahan to join the faculty of the Naval War College. Here, encapsulated in one document, is the basic difference between the modern fleet concept and the historical utilization of the U.S. Navy. Under Luce, the identity of the North Atlantic Squadron was that of a single combat unit, which sailed together, trained together, and expected to fight together. In short, the North Atlantic Squadron was an embryonic fleet, in the modern use of that word. To the State Department, however, and to a lesser extent the Navy Department, the North Atlantic Squadron was simply a collection of ships, from which the executive branch could draw upon as necessary to fulfill commitments to U.S. citizens, property, and business interests throughout their area of responsibility. While squadron exercises became commonplace, and even expected, throughout the decade of the 1880s, it was clear in 1888 that the new concepts had not yet been accepted as the basis of peacetime naval operations.

In any event, Luce did not have long to stew about his failure to convince the Navy Department of the validity of his views. Down in Haiti, the political unrest that had already deprived him of one of his ships earlier in the year had taken a turn for the worse. The *Haytian Republic*, a steamer flying the U.S. flag, was seized by the Haitian government. This was a clear violation of the international rights of U.S. citizens, and one that struck especially at the sensibilities of a United States always keenly interested in the protection of U.S. property abroad. On 8 December 1888, Luce was given back *Richmond* (temporarily) and told to take her and his remaining two ships *Galena* and *Yantic* and depart for Port-au-Prince at once. *Ossipee* would meet them on the way down, as they passed Norfolk. In the event, Luce accomplished the job with only *Galena* and *Yantic,* the other two vessels not being ready for sea fast enough. There is little doubt that Luce thought that there was a good possibility that hostilities would result, as he drilled his little command and made out battle instructions while in transit. The two ships would prove to be enough, however. They entered the harbor at Port-au-Prince at quarters, cleared for action with guns loaded. The provisional government, sensing that this was a fight that would be unprofitable for them, quickly released the *Haytian Republic.* In a letter to Secretary of the Navy Whitney, Secretary of State Bayard praised the "high and intelligent discretion which has characterized the action of Admiral Luce in the execution of this National duty to American citizens."

Conclusions

Luce applied for and received his detachment from the North Atlantic Squadron in January 1889. The decade of the 1880s had seen a change in the North Atlantic Squadron, not in structure or matériel, but in its sense of itself as an organization. As in any organization undergoing a fundamental change in image and identity, the squadron inhabited a middle ground between the old identity and the new. Although this characterization of the squadron's dual identity would be accurate until the middle of the 1890s, it was at no time truer than during the 1880s. The command tours of Rear Admiral Cooper and Rear Admiral Jouett bring this characterization into relief. Under Admiral Cooper's somewhat reluctant leadership, the squadron carried out at least four major sets of exercises, operating as a unit for a total of forty-four days. But the tactical exercises under Cooper were not part of an overall plan readying the squadron for combat as a tactical unit. They were products of opportunity that were dropped as events occurred that were determined to be more important to the squadron's critical function of showing the flag and protecting and promoting U.S. commerce. This is seen clearly in the command tour of Rear Admiral Jouett, who was only able to conduct a single week of tactical exercises, in April 1886. The highlight of his tenure as commander in chief was the revolution in

Colombia, an experience very much in keeping with the old Navy image of the naval officer as a warrior-diplomat.

After Rear Admiral Luce took command of the squadron in 1886, he brought a vision for an integrated training plan. Under his leadership, the North Atlantic Squadron warships not only trained together more often but did so as part of an overall scheme linking the theoretical work of the Naval War College with practical preparation. A routine developed that sent the warships of the squadron north in the summer so that their officers could participate in the college's summer session then return to their ships to put into action theoretical concepts worked out in the classroom. After these summer exercises, the squadron could send warships north to the Canadian fishing waters or south to the Caribbean. Its identity was becoming more that of a fighting unit and training organization and less that of an administrative body that facilitated assignment of ships to individual missions by the Navy Department. Years before Mahan popularized the theory of sea power, the operational patterns of the North Atlantic Squadron were laying the foundations for the development of a national battle fleet.

This vision was only partially realized in the 1880s. The decade to come would bring not only matériel changes with the arrival of the first of the steel ships of the New Steel Navy but also changes in the way those ships were employed. It would also bring to the forefront a powerful, politically connected officer who shared Luce's vision for a well-trained fighting squadron. Under Rear Adm. John Grimes Walker, the Squadron of Evolution, consisting of the *Atlanta*, *Boston*, *Chicago*, and *Dolphin*, would tour Europe, showing the nations of the Old World that the naval power of the United States was in the process of rebirth.

7 SELECTIONS FROM "AMERICAN NAVAL POLICY"

CDR Bradley A. Fiske, USN

Fiske wrote one hundred and ten years before Rentfrow, but he described the same need to improve fleet tactics. In 1905 Fiske was writing about our new battleship-centric Navy. He saw the ships and their tactics as the means to support American policy's ends. Even though his Navy was smaller than it is now, it was a big elephant that did not like to change its direction abruptly.

I selected Fiske, at that time a commander, as representative of the intense thinking about tactics in the U.S. Navy that went on at the beginning of the twentieth century, when the Naval Institute fostered better tactics and technology. I have seen nothing recently to compare with "American Naval Policy" in any military journal, *Proceedings* included. Among many useful writings on tactics, Fiske's comprehensive approach still stands out. His long article won the *Proceedings* General Prize as best essay of 1905.

Fiske starts with his personal premises of what is or soon will be American naval policy. Then he names the kinds of ships to compose an American fleet that best supports the policy. He examines in rich quantitative detail the characteristics of the ships: speed, endurance, gun size, and armor if the ship is a capital ship (a battleship or armored cruiser). Fittingly enough, Fiske demonstrates the advantages of the largest feasible battleship design because a large ship could be rugged enough to sustain damage and keep fighting, and because at the time a battleship's guns had to be big to penetrate an enemy's thick armor protection. In conclusion, he devotes a good quarter of his long essay to the best tactics to employ in the ships he espouses in support of American policy. The section of the essay that follows illustrates his highly focused and quantitative approach to fleet tactical readiness. It is as relevant now as when he wrote it. A first impression might be that Fiske was needlessly wordy. I've come to admire his plain-spoken style and absence of waffling.

One example of Fiske's enduring relevance should suffice. He predicts torpedoes will soon have longer ranges and higher speeds, "[a]nd, as it will be possible for nations to keep secret what they are doing in this way, there will be interjected into naval tactics a new complication. . . ." That is exactly what happened in 1942 during the fighting in the waters near Guadalcanal when the Japanese navy surprised the American navy with bigger, faster, longer-ranged "Long Lance" torpedoes fired in deadly salvoes at our columns, just as Fiske predicted. The only difference was that their targets were American cruisers and destroyers instead of battleships. Our ships and our tactical commanders were not, as Fiske insisted, trained for night surface actions. We didn't adapt sound tactics until the arrival of Admiral Ainsworth, Admiral Merrill, Commander Burke, and Commander Moosbrugger in early 1943, when the battles shifted to the upper Solomons. Are our ships and commanders ready for big or small fleet actions today, whether they are battles fought in the littoral waters like the Solomon Islands or by carrier battle groups operating in deep water in a variety of tactical situations? If we substitute today's advances in missile technology for advances in torpedoes, then we can appreciate the continuing relevance of Fiske's advice.

My focus in this anthology is not on quantitative analysis, but it is necessary to briefly explain Fiske's reference to "Table I." It appears in a part of the essay that I have omitted in this abridgement. Table I illustrates the advantage of concentration on a portion of the enemy fleet. Fiske assumes 1,000 identical units of combat potential are imbedded in two opposing fleets. If both fleets fight with all their potential, then of course the result will be mutual annihilation. The surprise is when Fiske shows in Table I the great advantage when one side's entire force can concentrate on half of the enemy fleet while isolating the other 500 units of combat potential in any way that keeps them from participating. Using difference equations, he tables the results at each time-step in the engagement. He shows that when the first 500 enemy units are all destroyed the side fighting with 1,000 units still has 841 remaining, all of which can then turn upon the enemy's second 500. Fiske is demonstrating the "Square Law" advantage of numerical superiority conceived by Frederick W. Lanchester ten years later for aerial combat. Moreover, a naval battle fits the square law conditions better than aerial combat does, unlike what Lanchester predicted. By time-stepping the battle, Fiske shows in Table I, and his other tables of which I have included only two, how even a small initial advantage between similar individual fleets accumulates as the battle progresses. Readers who are familiar with Lanchester's method using differential equations can compute that for Fiske's case of a two-to-one advantage, the winner would do even slightly better when both sides use "continuous" fire instead of salvoes as Fiske assumes. A Lanchester Square Law calculation would have shown the winner to have 866 units of combat potential remaining instead of 841 units. I have retained Tables V and VI to illustrate the "Lanchester square law" advantage described by Fiske for other tactical circumstances.

Bradley A. Fiske was a Navy renaissance man. By the time Fiske reached flag rank there was nothing he had not done. He was a skilled electrical engineer who designed the electrical motors and fire-control connections to make W. S. Sims' vision of continuous-aim fire a reality. He spent many years at sea where, several years before World War I and as a junior admiral, he was so taken with the potential of both the airplane and the torpedo that he designed and patented an aerial torpedo before Navy aircraft power plants were strong enough to lift a torpedo into the air! His essays, professional notes, and comments on the essays of others abound throughout the pages of *Proceedings*. A tour at the Naval War College broadened him as a strategist who tied effective policy to sound administration. He became frustrated with the organization of the Navy Department as an impediment to achieving a trained fighting force. He became a rebel who saw the need for, and was central in creating, the office of Chief of Naval Operations. Fiske also served as president of the U.S. Naval Institute for longer than anyone else.

SELECTIONS FROM "AMERICAN NAVAL POLICY"

By CDR Bradley A. Fiske, USN, U.S. Naval Institute *Proceedings* (January 1905): 46–64.

. . . If the fleets are so near the land that its nearness must be taken into account, the problem may become complicated in the extreme. If the land be friendly, if his own harbors and monitors and submarine boats and forts be there, the commander-in-chief might not hesitate to get between it and the enemy, if it were not that he would heartily desire to get the enemy between it and him. But each fleet will try to be the offshore fleet; and this will clearly be the case, even if the land be neutral. An exception to this case would, of course, exist if either side wished to have a harbor of refuge under its lee.

The best position will evidently be gotten by the fleet that is the faster, unless the other fleet be the better handled; and even this rough sketching of the situation shows that, in the handling, there will be need for skill of the highest order on the part of the commander-in-chief, either in utilizing superior speed or in preventing the enemy from utilizing superior speed.

[1] In order so to dispose his ships that he can direct his gunfire and torpedo-fire most effectively at each instant, at the enemy as disposed at that instant, the commander-in-chief must take into principal account the strength and direction of the sunlight, sea and wind, as just discussed; but this part of his endeavor has to do less with the relation of his entire fleet to the enemy than with the relation of his individual ships to each other. And while it is clearly true that he must consider his whole fleet as a unit, it should not be forgotten that no commander-in-chief will probably ever have a fleet made up of units so perfectly homogeneous, that he can allow himself to neglect the peculiarities of individual ships. And, even if he could do so at the beginning of the fight, it is sure that he could not do so after ships here and there had begun to get injured and disabled, both in his own fleet and in the enemy's fleet. Here will be room for admiralship of the highest order. How shall he strengthen his line, where it is beginning to waver? Shall he stop his column, because the Kearsarge is disabled; or shall he leave her, or shall he send the Kentucky to her aid, or shall he send a flotilla of torpedo-boats? What formation shall he direct, if about to be flanked or *T*'d; shall he change front or charge through the enemy's column, or try to ram? Shall he try to fight at long range or at short range? Shall he concentrate on individual ships, or allow each ship to fire at her opposite? Shall he use ahead fire, or beam fire or bow fire? Shall he dare to retreat a moment, if he thinks it would be wise; or shall he refrain, lest he be court-martialed afterwards for cowardice?

Although the commander-in-chief will have many formations at his command, in which to advance, retreat or jockey, there are only two in which he can fight with full battery power, and these are column and echelon, or line of bearing; and only one in which the gun, ram and torpedo can act together, and this is line.

Column is, of course, the easiest formation, and the one in which the most guns can be used. It has the disadvantages that the ships are helpless against the ram, unless they turn, and thereby destroy the column; and that, if the enemy be abeam, as it probably would be if the fleet were in column, each ship exposes the maximum length of water-line to the gun-fire and the maximum target to torpedo-fire. Now, if any ship in a column gets hit by a torpedo, or by a twelve-inch capped projectile at her water-line, her injury will probably affect not only herself, but the entire fleet; because the entire fleet will either have to abandon her, or slow down for her, or detach other ships to help her. In other words, a serious injury to the water-line of any ship, while it may not injure the offensive power of that ship so much as would the hitting of one of her turrets, may damage the whole fleet more than would the entire destruction of two of her turrets.

Echelon has the advantages that the guns and torpedoes can be fired nearly as effectively as if the fleet were in column, and that the fleet can, at the same time, close in or withdraw. For the sake of brevity, which is necessary in an article so short that attempts so much, echelon is here intended to mean any formation in which the ships are not in either line or column, but are on a line of bearing different from the course that they are heading. The main disadvantage of this formation is the difficulty of maintaining it; but it is clear that this trouble can be overcome by the simple expedients of practicing it, of taking careful note of compass deviations, of taking careful note of any changes in the speed curves, and of regulating the engine speeds to the necessary fraction of a revolution per minute.

The ideal fighting formation would be line, because the advance is in the direction of fire, and gun, ram and torpedo all can be used; were it not for the presentation of the long horizontal target of thin decks along the line of the enemy's fire; for the fact, at least in our service, that the ships do not have much fire ahead; and for the additional fact that the movement of the ships, if it be not directed at the enemy, gives the enemy a chance to flank; while if it be directed at the enemy, it will be apt to precipitate a mêlée, in which, both fleets having got close together, their guns, rams and torpedoes will combine in an indiscriminate slaughter of everybody.

If both fleets are nearly matched in speed and manageability and in the personal skill of the commander-in-chief, it would seem probable that neither fleet will be able to get a distinct advantage over the other in position. This being the case, and it being also the case that both commanders will recognize the loss in gun-hits that would follow every change of formation, or even turning of a ship, it seems probable that both fleets may "line up" in parallel columns, head to sea, just outside of effective torpedo range, and steam ahead as fast as they can; and that each commander will approach or withdraw, as seems best to him, from time to time, by changing the course very slightly towards the enemy, or away from him, but not the line of bearing.

As this operation, if gently done, will not interfere perceptibly with the gun-fire, and yet will give perfect opportunity for gradual advance, or retreat, and as it is a very difficult thing to do, even on drill, and with the officer of the deck on the bridge where he can see everything; and as the officer of the deck could not stay long there in battle, we see that *our battle-fleet should practice thoroughly at steaming in this formation, with the same officer controlling the ship who would control her in a fleet battle, and occupying the same place that he would occupy in a fleet battle.* There is only one way in which to get ready for any performance; and that is to rehearse it before hand, under conditions as nearly as possible like those under which the performance will eventually be given.

It may be pointed out here that the range and speed of the torpedo are about to be increased enormously. And, as it will be possible for nations to keep secret what they are doing in this way, there will be interjected into naval tactics a new complication, caused by lack of knowledge by an admiral as to how far he must keep away from the enemy, in order to be beyond his torpedo range. This factor is sure to become very important in time.

[2] In order to put his fleet into such formations as to present the least possible effective target to the gun-fire and torpedo-fire of the enemy, it is clear

that the commander-in-chief must refrain, so far as the desirability of attempting to get certain advantages will permit, from presenting the whole length of the water-line of his ships to the gun- and torpedo-fire of the enemy; and especially must avoid disposing his ships in such a way that a shell or torpedo fired at one ship will have a good chance of hitting some other ship.

Admiralship.—As the opposing commander-in-chief will try to force him into positions which he ought to avoid; and as such endeavors, if skillfully made, will not be apparent to an unskilled person until too late, we can easily see how wary and keen our admiral must be, not easily deceived by any feint; how well he must know every move on the ocean chess board; how familiar to him must be the peculiarities of every ship and every captain, not only in his own fleet, but, if possible, in the enemy's fleet; how he must *think* in fleets, and guns, and torpedoes, and turning circles, and range, and coal, and ammunition, and wind, and sea; in order that all mental operations involving them will be quick and sure; in order that he may handle his fleet with the same degree of quickness and accuracy as that which each gun-captain handles his gun.

Concentration and Isolation.—If one of the hostile fleets is concentrated and has an offensive power that can be called 1000; while the other fleet is in two parts of 500 each; and if the large force concentrate on one of the small forces and isolates it, Table I shows that, under the conditions named in Table I, it will have 841 left when the first small force is reduced to zero, and will have 841 ready to engage the other force of 500. But if it does not isolate one, but simply concentrates on one, while both fire at him, the result will be as indicated in Table V; showing that the aggregate of the values of the smaller forces will always remain equal to the larger force in this case, and that there is no advantage in concentration alone.

Table V

		A concentrates on B; B and C fire on A, until B is destroyed. A then fires at C. B and C fire at A.		A distributes his fire on B and C equally. B and C fire at A.		
Value of offensive power at beginning	A	1000			1000	
	B	500	1,000.00		500	1,000.00
	C	500			500	
Damage done in 1st period by	A				50	100.00
		100		To B " C	50	
	B	50	100.00		50	100.00
	C	50			50	
Value of offensive power at end 1st period	A	900			900	
	B	400	900.00		450	900.00
	C	500			450	
Damage done in 2d period by	A				45	90.00
		90		To B " C	45	
	B	40	90.00		45	90.00
	C	50			45	
Value of offensive power at end 2d period	A	810			810	
	B	310	810.00		405	810.00
	C	500			405	
Damage done in 3d period by	A			To B " C	40.5	81.00
		81			40.5	
	B	31	81.00		40.5	81.00
	C	50			40.5	
Value of offensive power at end of 3d period	A	729			729	
	B	229	729.00		364.5	729.00
	C	500			364.5	
Damage done in 4th period by	A			To B " C	36.5	73.00
		73			36.5	
	B	23	73.00		36.5	73.00
	C	50			36.5	
Value of offensive power end 4th period	A	656			656	
	B	156	656.00		328	656.00
	C	500			328	
Damage done in 5th period by	A			To B " C	33	66.00
		66			33	
	B	16	66.00		33	66.00
	C	50			33	
Value of offensive power end of 5th period	A	590			590	
	B	90	590.00		295	590.00
	C	500			295	
Damage done in 6th period by	A			To B " C	29	59.00
		59			30	
	B	29	59.00		29	59.00
	C	30			30	
Value of offensive power end 6th period	A	531			531	
	B	31	531.00		266	531.00
	C	500			265	

		A concentrates on B; B and C fire on A, until B is destroyed. A then fires at C. B and C fire at A.			A distributes his fire on B and C equally. B and C fire at A.		
Damage done in 7th period by	A	To B " C	31		To B " C	26	53.00
			22			27	
	B		3	53.00		26	53.00
	C		50			27	
Value of offensive power end 7th period	A		478			478	
	B			478.00		240	478.00
	C		478			238	
Damage done in 8th period by	A				To B " C	24	48.00
			48			24	
	B			48.00		24	48.00
	C		48			24	
Value of offensive power end 8th period	A		430			430	
	B			430.00		216	430.00
	C		430			214	
Damage done in 9th period by	A				To B " C	21	43.00
			43			22	
	B			43.00		21	43.00
	C		43			22	
Value of offensive power end 9th period	A		387			387	
	B			387.00		195	387.00
	C		387			192	
Damage done in 10th period by	A				To B " C	19	38.00
			38			19	
	B			38.00		19	38.00
	C		38			19	
Value of offensive power end 10th period	A		349			349	
	B			349.00		176	349.00
	C		349			173	
Damage done in 11th period by	A				To B " C	18	35.00
			35			17	
	B			35.00		18	35.00
	C		35			17	
Value of offensive power end 11th period	A		314			314	
	B			314.00		158	314.00
	C		314			156	
Damage done in 12th period by	A				To B " C	16	31.00
			31			15	
	B			31.00		16	31.00
	C		31			15	
Value of offensive power end 12th period	A		283			283	
	B			283.00		142	283.00
	C		283			141	
				etc.			

We may accept it as a principle there, that *concentration without isolation is nil.* Attention is here invited to Table VI.

Table VI			
Value offensive power beginning	A	970	569
	B	800	200
Damage done in 1st period by	A	97	57
	B	80	20
Value offensive power end 1st period	A	890	549
	B	703	143
Damage done in 2d period by	A	89	55
	B	70	14
Value offensive power end 2d period	A	820	535
	B	614	88
Damage done in 3d period by	A	82	54
	B	61	9
Value offensive power end 3d period	A	759	526
	B	532	32
Damage done in 4th period by	A	76	53
	B	53	3
Value offensive power end 4th period	A	706	523
	B	456	0
Damage done in 5th period by	A	71	...
	B	46	...
Value offensive power end 5th period	A	660	...
	B	385	...
Damage done in 6th period by	A	66	...
	B	39	...
Value offensive power end 6th period	A	621	...
	B	319	...
Damage done in 7th period by	A	62	...
	B	32	...
Value offensive power end 7th period	A	589	...
	B	257	...
Damage done in 8th period by	A	59	...
	B	26	...
Value offensive power end 8th period	A	563	...
	B	198	...
Damage done in 9th period by	A	56	...
	B	20	...
Value offensive power end 9th period	A	543	...
	B	142	...
Damage done in 10th period by	A	54	...
	B	14	...
Value offensive power end 10th period	A	529	...
	B	88	...
Damage done in 11th period by	A	53	...
	B	9	...
Value offensive power end 11th period	A	520	...
	B	35	...
Damage done in 12th period by	A	35	...
	B	3	...
Value offensive power end 12th period	A	517	...
	B	0	...

Undeveloped State of Naval Tactics.—A little reflection may lead us to believe that our ships which have been built, and which are building now, are such that they can be used pretty well to carry out any probable scheme of tactics. Many officers think that armored cruisers, as at present constructed, are not worth much, and that the changes back and forth in our ideas about battleships show that our policy has not rested on strategical principles, but on the personal "opinions" of men who have happened to come into power from time to time. This matter will be referred to again; but meantime it can be stated with truth that most officers believe that our ships, as merely ships, are very good; that the constructors and engineers have done their part well. If it be assumed that the ships, as ships, are good, we may inquire whether we have given sufficient study to the question of handling them in fleets; whether we have given sufficient study to what may be called *"admiralship."*

One could write a long book, and it would be a very interesting one, on the requirements of the officer who will handle our battle-fleet in the war that is to be. Even a brief abstract of such a book cannot be attempted here; though the rough sketch just given of two hostile fleets in each other's presence on the sea must suggest, not only that the infinity of possible situations and changes give opportunity for very great skill in admiralship, and that no more sublime field for exercising skill can be opened up to mortal man; but that, if we are to whip in our fleet fight, and not be whipped, we must develop admiralship to its highest attainable point.

Now there is no such word as "admiralship." There is such a word as "seamanship," and we hear it often in the navy. There is also such a word as "generalship;" and no word in the English language conveys a nobler thought; no word expresses a higher idea of the power a single man can wield. Surely no thoughtful officer can feel that the admiral who will command our fleet in war will have less need for skill in fleet handling than a general has for skill in army handling, or that fleet handling is easier than army handling. And while one may feel that the essential qualities and principles of admiralship are the same as those of generalship, he will recognize the fact that the conditions of handling fleets are so different from the conditions of handling armies, that the science and the art of admiralship must be developed as entirely distinct from generalship; just as distinct as they are from seamanship.

When one considers the enormous amount of literature that exists on the subject of military tactics, and compares it with the meager lot of literature on the subject of naval tactics; and when he contrasts the assured position that the principles of military tactics enjoy with the vagueness within which the principles of naval tactics seem to exist, the feeling must come to his mind that the science of naval tactics is in its infancy. And when he compares the vast mimic battles undertaken to practice armies in war, with the relatively pitiful little drills and search problems in which fleets engage, he must feel that the art of naval tactics has hardly yet been born. The comparison is nowhere clearer than in the way in which military men protect the general, compared with the way in which naval men expose the admiral. Military men recognize the fact that it would be absolutely impossible to replace a disabled general in battle without tremendous loss; that he, and only he, has the battle in hand; consequently they put the general in a place of comparative safety, from which he can exercise control of his forces as a whole. But naval men put the ship of the commander-in-chief and all his staff in the place where it has the maximum chance of being disabled and left, helpless and useless, behind the rest of the fleet, which must continue to advance, or be flanked.

Reasons for the Present Undeveloped State of Naval Tactics.—The reasons why the development of naval tactics has lagged so far behind the development of military tactics are not hard to find. A short reflection shows us that they are:

(1) The fact that the conditions of warfare on the land have changed very much less than the conditions of warfare on the sea. The principal factors in warfare on the land are the ground, the men and the weapons; of these, the ground and the men have remained the same, and the weapons have not changed very much. The principal factors in warfare on the sea are the water, the men and the weapons; of these the water and the men have remained the same; but the weapons have changed so much and so fast, and continue to change so much and so fast, that

naval tactics have not, thus far, been changed nimbly enough to keep up with them.

(2) Military tactics are so much more easily understood by civilians than are naval tactics, that military tactics have been assisted more in their development by men not soldiers than have naval tactics by men not sailors.

(3) Both military tactics and naval tactics need, for their systematic development, a good deal of writing; because, at the present day, no art can be developed without the co-working of many people. And writers on military tactics, being for the most part together on the land, have better facilities for formulating their systems than have writers on naval tactics, who have to be, for the most part, widely separated on the sea.

(4) The mental work required of army officers in the exercise of their ordinary duties is so much less than that required of naval officers in the exercise of their ordinary duties, that they have more time and energy left for the study of tactics. The duties of army officers below the rank of brigadier-general are very simple; so simple that they have often been exercised with splendid skill by men of very little military training, or even common education. But the duties of naval officers, of even the earliest ranks, call into constant exercise mental activity of the most rigorous kinds, involving often momentous results.

(5) In most navies, and especially in our navy, the responsibilities of an officer are mostly limited to one part of one ship, until he reaches command rank. In our navy, command rank is attained, on the average, at about the age of fifty-one. Up to this time, the officer's responsibility is fully occupied with questions minor in general importance to tactics, but not minor in importance to him personally; because his personal responsibility, and even his life, are concerned in them. Between the ages of fifty-one and sixty-two, the responsibilities of an officer are usually limited to one ship, unless he is promoted to flag rank. This rank, if attained at all, is attained at about the age of sixty; so that between the ages of fifty-one and sixty, the responsibilities of most officers are

limited to one ship. Since officers of our service retire at the age of sixty-two, we know that only from the age of sixty to the age of sixty-two, if ever, shall we have any responsibility connected with naval tactics, except in managing one ship in obedience to signal. Now, we all know that the admirable automatic mechanism put inside every human being by nature may be relied on to regulate his life in ways where his own responsibility and safety are concerned; but that it does not make him do much work, either physical or mental, that does not have some close relation to his own personal life.

(6) In the case of the American navy, the ships and methods were allowed after the Civil War, not merely to cease to keep up with the advance of civilization in other arts, but actually to revert to more ancient conditions still. The result was that, when reconstruction began in 1881, we were so far behind, that we have not even yet succeeded in getting our ships to equal those of nations who always kept up in naval matters; and the changes in ships and mechanisms have been so rapid and tremendous, that officers, especially officers of the flag rank and command rank, whose professional education was almost wholly confined to sails and spars, have had all they could do to learn to manage the ships and their mechanisms, and have had to leave the larger, but less urgent, questions of naval tactics to those who should come after. And let this not be laid to their discredit. The elaborate scientific mechanisms of a battleship may seem easy to learn to the young officer educated specially and directly for it by the Naval Academy; but he cannot even imagine the efforts that have had to be put forth to master them by officers, already mature, whose minds at the receptive age were filled with sails and spars, and whose total education in electricity was comprised in a few chapters on frictional machines, the voltaic cell and the Leyden jar.

(7) But the main reason, the all-sufficient reason, why there is almost no such thing as naval tactics, is the persistence of the idea, which comes from barbarous times, that the commander-in-chief should be on the

fighting line. Armies got rid of this idea long ago. In barbarous times, a general used to lead a charge or an assault; but, even then, when the direction of large forces was required, custom put the general where he could exercise the functions of a general, and direct. Why do not we put the admiral where he can exercise the functions of an admiral and direct, or at least, see? Armies have had ten thousand times as much experience in fighting as navies; why cannot navies learn from them? There is absolutely no use in trying to learn how to direct a fleet in battle so long as the admiral is put where he cannot possibly direct. Farragut had to be lashed aloft, in order to direct. *Yet, in forty years, we have drawn no lesson from this well-known fact.* And there is no difficulty whatever in putting the admiral where he can direct. We have simply to give him a ship like the Colorado, made into a proper flagship by the simple plan of putting into her lofty signal masts and observing stations, and securing on her water-line a belt of twelve-inch armor. The weight can be made permissible by taking off the six-inch guns and side armor. The expense will be considerable; but this expense ought not to be charged against this beneficent change, but against the original plan of the ship, which made the change necessary.

It may be argued that our forefathers got along very well with the flagship on the battle line. True; but they got along very well without the sewing machine or the telephone.

Development of a System of Tactics.—If this is to be carried out successfully, it is clear that the problem of how to carry it out must be attacked as a definite thing; on the principle that it is really the naval problem, par excellence, and that all details of drill and discipline must be directed to carrying it out; not that it shall be directed by details of drill and discipline. Without any intention of criticising the policy that has directed the navy until recent years, and recognizing fully the enormous work that had to be done in building up the "new navy," it does seem that, in many ways, our policy has been shaped along the line of the least resistance, and has been made to conform to old ideas of drill and discipline, instead of modifying old ideas to conform to it. In Germany and Japan, on the contrary, the "new navy" started on broad principles that had been proved to be good, and was really *new*; old customs and ideas that were not of practical use, were ignored, and the "new navy" went ahead unfettered. In the British navy, there has never been any dividing line between the old navy and the new navy; because the British navy was always kept moving along a healthy line of progress, and ships and ideas that had become obsolete were replaced continually by ships and ideas that were not obsolete. But even in the British navy, there has been a continual warfare between the conservative and the progressive men; and a very healthy effect it has had, in preventing the bad effects of extremism on both sides. But the British navy has, nevertheless, been handicapped by obsolete things; and it is, in this way, at a disadvantage with the navies of Germany and Japan, who were able to start fresh with everything new. In our navy, we have been just as much handicapped by tradition and custom as the British navy; and our predecessors in office, assisted by Congress, after the Civil War and until 1881, let the navy get into such a miserable state, not only in ships and guns, but in professional aims and standards, that we have had a hard time to breathe into its nostrils the breath of life. . . .

It is clear that there are three important ways in which we have already broken away from too rigid an adherence to "the traditions of the service":

(1) We have broken away from obsolete types of ships and guns, and have in use new types of ships and guns that are fitted, in a measure, to fight against the ships and guns of probable enemies.

(2) We have an improved morale: a spirit in officers, in men, that takes an interest in the service as a living thing; a spirit that makes officers and men take pride in their ships and guns, and feel the brotherly spirit which always exists among men who are working together to a common end; a spirit that recognizes the fact that, barring occasional lapses, nearly every officer and man in the service, no matter what his station, really wants to do his duty well. This improved morale is largely due to—

(3) The healthy and exciting emulation in gunnery brought about by Sims, supported by the President, and the amazing practical improvement that has resulted.

But, has our system of tactics improved as much as our ships, guns, morale and gunnery? It is not necessary to answer this question aloud; but let each officer who can remember a time so long ago, recall the fleet maneuvers under Admiral Luce in 1889, and compare them with those of the present time; let him compare the signal books used then and now, and answer the question, very quietly, to himself.

There may be some officers who think that our system of tactics has not improved so much as these other things. Assuming, for the sake of the interest of the subject, that they are right, the question comes up at once, how shall we improve it?

Having had so recent and startling an instance of improvement as our improvement in target practice, the answer at once suggests itself that, because Sims improved our target practice by concentrating our energies on it, perhaps we can develop a system of naval tactics by concentrating our energies on it.

Assuming that we are to concentrate our energies on the development of a system of naval tactics, it would seem that the things to do are to:

(1) Form the battle-fleet.
(2) Organize it into sections, divisions and squadrons, with appropriate auxiliaries.
(3) Drill it—first, as individual ships; second, in sections; third, in divisions; fourth, in squadrons; fifth, as a unit fleet. It is plain that 1 and 2 can easily be done, because the only thing needed is an executive order. But in order to carry out 3 wisely, many obstacles must be overcome. The most difficult obstacles, perhaps, are:

(a) The long intervals during which battleships are kept in navy yards for repairs, during which intervals officers and men get out of practice.

(b) The fact that some ships begin to show defects in boilers, engines, or other mechanisms, after being a few weeks away from the yard; thus handicapping the entire fleet.

(c) The difficulty of keeping up the interest of officers and men in any mere drill, combined with the fact that no good scheme of naval tactics can be developed without their interest.

These difficulties seem very big; but it may be pointed out that the great ocean liners go regularly across the ocean, year after year; and that, if we could find out how they do it, we might entirely avoid obstacles [a] and [b]. Now, every one knows that these liners *make repairs at the end of every trip*. The thought suggests itself, "suppose that we used our battleships as hard as possible for one week, then repaired them for two weeks; then used them for another week, and repaired them for two weeks, and so forth. Could we not keep them always in repair, always ready, for ten years continuously?" Of course we could. Then why not do it? . . .

The idea now struggling for utterance is largely an amplification of that outlined by Lieutenant Fullenwider in his admirable prize essay of 1904; and it would seem not difficult of execution. Without pretending to have worked the idea into practical shape, it may be suggested that the weather near New York during the months of April, May, June, July, August, September, October and November is admirably fitted for fleet maneuvers. In these eight months, the fleet could concentrate for maneuvers at a place about fifty miles southeast of Sandy Hook, clear of the ordinary steamer routes. Here it could drill for five days and five nights at fleet maneuvers of all kinds, including wireless telegraphy with the shore. At the end, the squadrons could disperse; the first squadron of battleships going, say to Tompkinsville, the second to Hampton Roads, the torpedo flotilla to Newport, the cruisers to Boston, the auxiliaries to the mouth of the Delaware, and have two weeks clear for repairs and coaling. On the first of December, the entire fleet could go south, and make Pensacola, New Orleans, Key West, Tortugas and Galveston their home bases, assembling in the Gulf of Mexico for their maneuvers as the war-fleet for five days every three weeks. . . .

So, with our fleet, the way to develop a system of tactics is not to "work hard," but to get good ideas. Why not make the fleet work seem like war? Everyone in the world is interested in war. If we fight our squadrons together in sham battles, the stimulus of competition will bring out good ideas automatically. A system of tactics will develop itself; it will simply grow. Every officer will take the joyous interest in the battles that he takes in a game of football or a prize-fight.

And the enlisted men will be interested too; every man will feel that he is immediately concerned, one of the players; that he, Charles Noble, contributes something of his own personal skill and prowess to the result. There is no trouble in making men work if you can make the work interesting; but you can never make men do the best that is in them at mere drudgery. Now drudgery is not necessarily manual labor; manual labor, even shoveling coal, is not drudgery if the men doing the shoveling are trying to beat some other men, or trying to accomplish anything that they know about; and work of the most refined and artistic kind is drudgery if it is done without interest. *Interest makes the difference, and the only difference, between pleasant occupation and drudgery.*

Now, interest is a powerful factor in making men work; but it is a much more powerful factor in making men think. Who has not noticed that it is easier to teach children things that interest them than things that do not? A man can be compelled to do drudgery; but he cannot be compelled to think. He will, however, think unconsciously, if interested.

How interesting and thought-inducing it would be, if our fleets should be practiced continually in team work, and the practice be of a kind that would show every one exactly what its meaning was! While the carrying out of any maneuver, even of the simplest kind, requires technical skill, the bottom principles of warfare are very simple, and are curiously like those of baseball and football, and other games in which pluck and drill are needed. The most ordinary "rooter " knows which side is playing a baseball game the better, though he may himself be unable to hit a ball, or catch it.

So, if we fight our fleets in mimic fights against each other, every officer, and seaman, and fireman, and ward-room boy will understand enough to become interested. What we need more than anything else is to make our people *interested*. Any one who is interested is very close to being happy. And certainly no profession gives the opportunities for continued interest that ours does. No profession equals it in dramatic situations and picturesque scenes. Yet is there anything more heartbreaking in its dullness than a man-of-war is often made to be!

If, then, it be found practicable to form a battle-fleet and drill it on our coast in the way outlined, we see that the following advantage will result:

(1) A system of naval tactics will be developed at sea; not in an office.

(2) Engines, boilers, and other mechanisms can be kept in constant repair.

(3) Suggestions for improvements in mechanisms and methods can be tested at once, reported on at once, and adopted at once, if good.

(4) Nearly every question of drill, policy, strategy or tactics can be tested and decided correctly, instead of being merely talked about and written about. We shall cease to hear long disputes about the tactical value of speed, because we can actually test the tactical value of speed; or as to how many ships can be handled together, or as to the best formations for attack. We can see all these things tested with our own eyes; and this is necessary, because most of us have not much imagination; we are like the old gentleman in one of Dickens's works, who could not talk about—was it Pip?—unless the child was brought into the room, and put directly in front of him.

(5) The fleet will, after—say a year—of systematic maneuvering, constitute a fighting force that can be handled like a unit.

(6) When it finally goes into battle, not only will the fleet be handled well, but the officers and men will be able to recognize the various phases the action will take on, by identifying them with similar phases that have come up in the sham battles; and will act with preparedness of mind, and therefore with presence of mind.

(7) Officers and men will lead a life of the greatest professional interest.

(8) The greatest disadvantage of naval life, the long and distant absences from home, will, so far as the great majority, the people in the battle-fleet,

are concerned, entirely be removed. Instead of interminable months in bad climates, with no mail, and nothing to do or think about, officers and men will be able to have occasional diversion, to be with their wives and sweethearts from time to time, and live like other men.

(9) But the main advantage, the all-sufficient advantage, will be that our battle-fleet will really be *always ready*. There will be no mobilization needed. There will be no sudden question about the Kearsarge's boilers, or the Alabama's forward turret, or the Missouri's engines. There will be no doubt about coal; no need for hasty action; no delay. A telephone message from the Department to the commandant of a certain district, a wireless message from his office, and the fleet will instantly be on a war footing.

8 "TIME IS EVERYTHING"

(Selection from chapter 16 of *Black Shoe Carrier Admiral*)

John B. Lundstrom

One of the best battles to study for tactical wisdom is Midway. The extract that follows is not about the battle, which Lundstrom describes in too much detail for an anthology. Instead, you will read about the circumstances before the battle and the personalities of our leaders. I regard Lundstrom's description as the fairest appraisal of all factors involved in the decisive American victory. Some historians have sought out blunders by the Japanese side to explain their defeat when their superiority, measured in warship numbers and displacements, seemed overwhelming. The Japanese made mistakes, but few battles are fought perfectly. It is far more instructive to discuss what it took for the outnumbered and less combat-experienced U.S. Navy to pull off its amazing victory. One does not need to point to Japanese errors to understand why we won. Six factors on the American side were necessary and sufficient:

—*Cryptanalysis.* We could read enough of the Japanese traffic to assemble the fleet and deploy it in time to ambush the Japanese. But what the code breakers deduced was not certainty. Admiral Chester

W. Nimitz had both the courage and the insight to act before all the returns were in.

—*Leadership.* Nimitz was his own tactical commander until the Japanese carriers were located. This was because our carriers had to stay invisible to Yamamoto; because only PACFLT could transmit and receive the communications for successful long-range air reconnaissance; and because only Nimitz could communicate openly to order attacks by our beefed-up air contingent on Midway Island.

—*Courage.* We honor the great physical courage in our pilots, especially in the torpedo bombers who were crucial to the victory. Great respect is also due the moral courage in our leaders, Nimitz, Fletcher, Spruance, and most of the air squadron commanders.

—*Luck.* That a Japanese scout was delayed long enough to be late in finding our carriers was a great good fortune, but it was not an unusual happening at this stage of the war. What was just plain dumb luck was that three squadrons of dive bombers arrived simultaneously above four Japanese carriers to fatally damage three of them within five minutes at 1025 on 4 June 1942.

—*Radar.* Our torpedo squadrons could not have drawn all forty-one Japanese combat air patrol down on the deck if Admiral Nagumo had had an air search radar equivalent to our own. Absence of radar was fatal.

—*Midway Island serving as a fourth carrier.* The irony here is that Admiral Nagumo forgot his primary purpose was to use Midway as a decoy to draw the inferior U.S. fleet into a decisive battle. He became overly enchanted with a successful invasion, with fatal consequences.

Anticipate these factors as you read how Nimitz deployed his forces. It is hard to find a more instructive battle to understand the challenges of tactical competency in 1942.

"TIME IS EVERYTHING"

(Selection from chapter 16 of *Black Shoe Carrier Admiral: Frank Jack Fletcher at Coral Sea, Midway, and Guadalcanal*) by John B. Lundstrom (Naval Institute Press, 2006): 222–36.

A Question of Command

On the afternoon of 27 May, after a cruise of 101 days, two raids, and a battle, Fletcher's TF-17 gathered at the narrow entrance of Pearl Harbor right on schedule. Its arrival was a surprise, because Cincpac had reckoned fuel shortage would delay its return until the twenty-eighth. The *Yorktown* still trailed oil from seams opened on 8 May. On the way in, her sailors noted the encouraging absence of the beached battleship *Nevada*, since refloated and dispatched to the West Coast, which was where they thought they, too, would shortly be. Off Ford Island loomed the *Enterprise* and *Hornet*. Nimitz happened to be on the *Big E* awarding decorations. He would have a great deal to say to Fletcher later that day. The *Yorktown* executed a clockwise turn around Ford Island. If the removal of the *Nevada* was a positive sign, the forlorn bow of the capsized *Utah*, the *Arizona*'s skeletal mainmast, and the vast flat bottom of the *Oklahoma* reminded all of the 7 December outrage. The *Yorktown* moved alongside Pier B-16 in the navy yard's repair basin, opposite the channel from the *Enterprise*.

Coming into Pearl, Fletcher felt an unsettling premonition about the *Yorktown*'s ultimate fate, but had no clear idea how that might occur. If a trip to Bremerton was not in the cards, she needed a couple of weeks to get patched up. A staff officer strode on board to tell Fletcher that Nimitz wished to see him. Already prepared for the usual arrival call to Cincpac, Fletcher thought he amply earned the right to a quick drink first and strolled ashore to get one. Then he collected Poco Smith, reported to headquarters at the submarine base, and found Nimitz and Draemel awaiting him. To Fletcher's surprise, Nimitz, "Normally the calmest of people," appeared "exceptionally disturbed." Asked how he felt after such a long, hard cruise, Fletcher replied, "Pretty tired." Smith wondered, "How long the old poops and even the young officers can stand the strain." Nimitz explained that under normal circumstances Fletcher and the *Yorktown* deserved a rest, but things were far from normal. "We have to fix you up right away and send you out to Midway." The mention of Midway took Fletcher aback. The intelligence he saw in the last several weeks contained no hint of danger there. Nimitz explained that Midway would be invaded in the next several days and added sarcastically the Japanese were so confident of victory, they already appointed the officer who was to take command there in August. He never explicitly stated this amazing intelligence was derived from breaking the enemy code. Fletcher already knew that was the case. Smith did not, but as one of the navy's early cryptographers, he quickly figured it out.

Nimitz followed the bombshell about the enemy's Midway offensive with shocking news that Bill Halsey was hospitalized after arriving the previous afternoon. Halsey's haggard features shook even Nimitz's legendary calm. Ever since February he suffered from unbearable itching all over his body due to "general dermatitis." The tremendous stress exacerbated an underlying allergic skin reaction and prevented him from getting rest. On the recent cruise to the South Pacific the fierce tropical sun forced Halsey to remain in his flag quarters, "Which irked him to no end." Capt. Miles Browning, chief of staff, and Cdr. William H. Buracker, operations officer, actually ran TF-16, with Halsey's "advice and concurrence." That could not continue. Now gaunt, shrunken, and exhausted, Halsey clearly was in no shape to fight. Missing Midway was to be "the most grievous disappointment" in his career.

Halsey's sudden illness threw Nimitz into a terrible quandary. He had counted on his most aggressive and experienced warrior to lead the carriers in their toughest battle, one that could decide the war in the Pacific. . . .

To Nimitz's surprise Halsey fervently recommended Rear Adm. Raymond Spruance (Comcrudiv Five), his cruiser task group commander, to succeed him as CTF-16. Indeed he declared Spruance was the only admiral to whom he would willingly entrust the two carriers. Halsey laid the foundation with a 25 May letter to Fletcher, who as Comcrupac was Spruance's superior. Halsey praised Spruance's "outstanding ability, excellent judgment, quiet courage" and declared he was "fully and supremely qualified to take command of a force comprising mixed types." On 26 May Halsey proposed Spruance retain the whole elite Carriers, Pacific Fleet (Carpac) staff; exchanging only flag lieutenants. Nimitz barely knew him but he was aware of Spruance's sterling reputation as a naval strategist. That would soon change, for Spruance was slated to relieve Draemel as Cincpac chief of staff. Earlier in May Nimitz wrote privately to King requesting the change, because Draemel, his principal planner, disagreed with his fundamental strategy. At the same time Wilson Brown's precarious health meant Draemel could relieve him as Pacific Fleet's amphibious commander. Spruance was a logical candidate for chief of staff. Like Draemel he had a strong background of study and teaching at the Naval War College and thoroughly understood the operational art. He also brought the benefit of recent combat experience. Trusting Halsey's judgment, Nimitz acceded, primarily, it appears, to ensure continuity of command within TF-16, rather than, as is so often stated in hindsight, from an underlying belief that Spruance might actually do better than Halsey at Midway. In 1965 Nimitz could say, "It was a great day for the Navy when Bill Halsey had to enter the hospital." He certainly did not think so at the time. He procrastinated until the evening of 27 May before informing King that Halsey was incapacitated by an "obscure allergy," and he had already named a successor to lead TF-16. A strong case can be made that Halsey's presence was sorely missed at Midway.

On the twenty-sixth Spruance repaired to the *Enterprise* to make his call on Halsey and found flag country unusually still. He learned Halsey had been admitted to the hospital and that Nimitz wanted to see him. Then Nimitz floored him by placing him in command of TF-16 for the defense of Midway. Afterward he would come ashore to run the Cincpac staff. Unlike Fletcher, Spruance already knew from high-level messages shared by Halsey that a battle for Midway was in the offing, but he was astonished at becoming CTF-16 in his boss's place. "Since I was not an aviator, and there were aviators senior to me at Pearl Harbor, I thought one of them would take over from Halsey." A 1907 Annapolis graduate, Spruance cut his teeth in destroyers and taught five years at the Naval War College, where he became renowned as a naval strategist. Promoted to rear admiral in 1940, he organized the Tenth Naval District in the Caribbean before taking Crudiv Five in September 1941. Age fifty-five, medium height and slender, with a quiet and contemplative disposition and an addiction to long walks, he was a brilliant thinker, an excellent seaman, and a "cold fish." Lt. Cdr. Victor D. Long, Crudiv Five flag secretary, described his boss as "essentially . . . a machine," who "had no emotions or didn't show them." Others, however, noted the twinkling eyes and the dry sense of humor. Spruance worshipped logic and order. He and Halsey were very close, although they were fire and ice. . . .

Therefore if, as it seemed likely, the *Yorktown* could fight, Fletcher would lead all the carriers at Midway. After explaining the TF-16 command situation to Fletcher and Smith, Nimitz discussed the *Yorktown*'s condition. Fletcher's arrival a day earlier than expected proved crucial. On 26 May War Plans hoped she might be ready to go in four days; otherwise an immediate trip to Bremerton was in order. Now from talking with Fletcher, Nimitz estimated the carrier should be ready in forty-eight to sixty hours. He directed she be brought into dry dock the next morning with the special (and risky) dispensation of not removing aviation gasoline beforehand. The navy yard was to complete hull repairs by 0630 on 29 May and refloat her to refuel. Thus Nimitz counted on Fletcher to depart on 30 May. Reestablishing her watertight integrity would be difficult in such a short time. The loading of ammunition, provisions, and supplies was to begin as soon as possible. The other ships would also require working day and night. Nimitz authorized liberty for the long-suffering TF-17 sailors. For Fletcher other news was not so good. Former *Saratoga* squadrons were replacing nearly all his trusted *Yorktown* aviators. . . .

The Midway Plan

At dinner Nimitz reconvened the conference that now included Fletcher, Spruance, Noyes, Draemel, and Smith, along with important staff. Having briefed senior army and navy commanders that morning, Nimitz again elucidated his ideas regarding the offensive against Midway and the Aleutians. He was superb in these prebattle conferences. Fletcher thought Nimitz was "rather shocked by the enormity of it all, but still he remained calm and imperturbable. These were his best characteristics." Spruance admired Nimitz's "intelligence, open-mindedness, approachability for anyone who had different ideas, and above all, his utter fearlessness and his courage in pushing the war." To Spruance "an offensive fighting spirit is of the utmost importance in the top commanders." Nimitz encouraged his subordinates through quiet confidence laced with humor not cheerleading histrionics or the coercion of a taskmaster.

Nimitz distributed Cincpac Operation Plan 29-42 that McCormick's War Plans Section just compiled. Against the Midway-Hawaii line, Japan could employ four or five big carriers, two to four fast battleships, and seven to nine cruisers with commensurate numbers of destroyers, up to two dozen submarines, and a powerful landing force. (Actual strength was even greater because of the participation of the First Fleet's battleships, hints of which the code breakers detected but which, for unexplained reasons, the analysts discounted.) Smaller but powerful forces, including carriers, threatened the Aleutians. The two offensives would commence shortly. Subs would first reconnoiter U.S. fleet dispositions and form blocking lines to catch ships that sortied to succor Midway. There might even be another night bombing of Pearl Harbor by flying boats, as in March. The carriers would close swiftly to overwhelm Midway's defense and open the way for invasion. King believed that "N-Day," when the Midway and Aleutian landings would take place, was 3 June, but Nimitz leaned toward 5 June (one day prior to the real N-Day). The initial carrier air attacks could begin on 3 or 4 June, likely from northwest of Midway, while heavy ships pounded the defenses at night. The landings themselves might occur at night. Should Midway fall, the Japanese would immediately rush in aircraft and base defenses to consolidate their hold. As for the Aleutians, Nimitz elected only to reinforce its shore-based aircraft and form TF-8 under Admiral Theobald, with two heavy cruisers, three light cruisers, and four destroyers. Nimitz made Midway his personal battle. Exercising "general tactical command" from Pearl, he positioned all of the forces and approved the search patterns.

What was available for Midway? Nimitz wisely ruled out the seven old, slow battleships of Pye's TF-1 based at San Francisco. They still lacked the vital air support and screening ships essential when battling forces supported by carriers. As usual King hoped to use the battleships, but Nimitz declared on 24 May that he would hold them on the West Coast "until objectives for their striking power are more definite." He thought in the back of his mind they could pummel Midway should he have to retake it. Eventually he hoped to use converted auxiliary carriers to protect the battleships, but now he had only the *Long Island*, the first U.S. auxiliary carrier. The *Saratoga* was far more valuable with the carrier striking force than shepherding old battleships. Such a passive role did not sit well with a restive Pye, who thought he should take an active role in the defense of Midway or at least the Hawaiian Islands.

Having dispensed with the battleships, Nimitz reckoned on four basic assets. Spruance's TF-16 (*Enterprise* and *Hornet*) would be in position off Midway by 1 June; TF-17 (*Yorktown*) would join the next day. Fletcher received tactical command of both task forces, which totaled 230 planes. Fitch's TF-11 (*Saratoga*) should depart San Diego on 5 June, too late to fight at Midway unless the Japanese were considerably delayed. Bellinger (CTF-9, shore-based aircraft) was to deploy as many navy, marine, and army aircraft onto Midway as the small atoll could comfortably hold. That ultimately numbered 125 planes under Capt. Cyril T. Simard, the island commander. Long-range searches by PBYs from Midway and Johnston would locate suitable targets, both for the carriers and land-based bombers that included B-17s shuttling in from Hawaii. Simard's marine fighters must defend the air base against certain fierce and unremitting air attack. A proud wearer of the submariner's dolphin insignia, Nimitz anticipated a stellar performance from Rear Adm. Robert H. English's Pacific Fleet subs (TF-7). A dozen boats would form a scouting line west of Midway, patrol their sectors until contact was made, then swarm in. All available subs would reinforce them. Finally, more than two thousand resolute, well-armed marines would defend Midway itself.

Weaker than his opponents in most categories, Nimitz could no longer simply meet them head-on. McCormick put it well. "Not only the directive from [Cominch] but also common sense dictates that we cannot now afford to slug it out with the probably superior approaching Japanese forces." Instead, "We must endeavor to reduce his forces by attrition—submarine attacks, air bombing, attacks on isolated units." Thus, "If attrition is successful the enemy must accept the failure of his venture or risk battle on disadvantageous terms for him." McCormick took notice of King's all-too-accurate fear that the Japanese intended to trap the surface forces but thought the extensive air reconnaissance should forestall that calamity. It was vital to get the maximum effect out of Midway's air, "Without exposing our carriers to danger of destruction out of proportion to the damage they can inflict. We must calculate the risk and must accept the danger when our prospects of frustrating or destroying the enemy carriers are sufficiently good."

Nimitz looked carefully into the deployment of his carriers, the key to success at Midway. As excellent as radio intelligence was in predicting Japanese strategic intentions, he had relatively little actual information, other than his own common sense, as to how the enemy might go about reducing Midway. An important clue from a decrypt appeared in Layton's scorecard on 21 May. "Staff member 1st Air Fleet request [*sic*] weather data from 3 hrs. prior to take off on 'N'-2 day. Asked to be informed of any BLUE activity that area. Planes will be launched 50 miles N.W. of Midway attacking from N–2 days until N-day." Thus Nimitz deduced that for two days prior to the invasion the whole carrier force would strike Midway "from short range, say 50 to 100 miles," to pulverize its air defenses. Midway's own planes "must try to inflict prompt early damage to Jap carrier flight decks if recurring attacks are to be stopped." Nimitz tasked Davis, his fleet aviation officer, to "visualize as closely as possible [the Japanese] method of operation and OUR best counter tactics." He wanted Davis to keep in mind, "Where does Halsey best fit into this picture, remembering we can ill afford loss of carriers." It was vital to determine the best initial position for the U.S. carriers. Nimitz had previously directed Bellinger to fashion a search pattern that would find the enemy carriers before they could close Midway. Bellinger explained, "Each day's search must cover enemy movements to such a distance that the next day's search will reach the enemy carrier's probable launching radius before he can reach it." Thus he proposed a dawn search by the PBYs to seven hundred miles.

Replying on 26 May, Davis warned Nimitz that "unless early, and preferably advance, serious damage is done to enemy CVs," Midway's aircraft would have little effect. Bellinger's suggested long-range search offered "the best chance for us to get in the first effective blows, not only with Midway planes but also with both our carrier planes and our submarines." The proposed pattern of searches from Midway and Johnston "will leave an excellent flanking area northeast of Midway for our carriers. With prompt action by both carriers and submarines, these forces should best be able to do their stuff." Davis stressed it was "particularly important that the carriers be able to take action at the earliest possible moment." Bellinger's search plan "should make it practicable for our carriers to be reasonably close to Midway and thus in position for early action when opportunity arises." Therefore, "Our supporting CVs should be close in for best chance of success, and the full VP [flying boat] search will justify this."

Nimitz agreed that the sector northeast of Midway was the best initial location for his carrier striking force. From there the carriers could "seize opportunity to obtain initial advantage against carriers which are employing their air groups against Midway." The goal was to "inflict maximum damage on enemy by employing strong attrition tactics," but "not accept such decisive action as would be likely to incur heavy losses in our carriers and cruisers." Cincpac's separate letter of instruction to Fletcher and Spruance directed them to "be governed by the principle of calculated risk which you shall interpret to mean the avoidance of exposure of your forces to attack by superior enemy forces without good prospect of inflicting, as a result of such exposure, greater damage to the enemy. This applies to a landing phase as well as during preliminary air attacks." Spruance's flag lieutenant, Robert J. Oliver, recalled that Nimitz told Spruance no matter what not to lose his carriers. If things got too rough, he was to withdraw and let Midway fall. Any enemy foothold so far east could be recaptured later. Fletcher doubtless received the same instructions.

The defense of Midway posed a daunting task. The Japanese "have amply demonstrated their ability to use their carrier air with great ability," and "we can no longer underestimate their naval air efficiency." That is a rather surprising admission that showed that prior to the loss of the *Lexington*, Japanese prowess was not recognized. Nimitz's decision to fight at Midway was all the more courageous. Japan held the initiative. The Combined Fleet outnumbered the Pacific Fleet in all classes of combat ships. Its carrier aircraft enjoyed longer range and the fighters possibly superior performance. Its amphibious forces were experienced and highly efficient. The weaker Pacific Fleet must resort to attrition tactics rather than direct confrontation. Yet Nimitz had strong reason for optimism at Midway. The situation certainly warranted taking a "calculated risk." His men were "just as brave, and those who have been properly trained are believed to be better than their opposite Jap number." The remarkable radio intelligence gave him sufficient warning to gather his forces in secret. Japan must expose its precious carriers to counterattack vastly abetted by the element of surprise. The enemy would confront a "fairly strong" land-based air force beyond supporting range of his own shore-based aviation. "Our submarines have demonstrated considerable superiority." The assault on Midway would prove costly to the attackers. The battle was far from the desperate gamble that is often portrayed. Although the odds still favored Japan, Nimitz had devised a careful plan where victory would pay enormous dividends. . . .

Fletcher was understandably apprehensive over losing most of his highly valued veteran aviators. On the afternoon of 27 May the Carpac administrative office ordered Burch's Scouting Five, Taylor's Torpedo Five, and Fenton's Fighting Forty-two detached from the *Yorktown* Air Group. They were to draw replacement pilots and planes and embark in the *Saratoga* in the next ten days. The only remaining original *Yorktown* squadron was Lieutenant Short's Bombing Five. Joining the group were the three *Saratoga* squadrons stranded at Pearl since February. Only Lt. Cdr. Maxwell F. Leslie's Bombing Three had recent carrier time, having gone with the *Enterprise* on the Tokyo raid. Lt. Cdr. Lance E. Massey's Torpedo Three was green. Lt. Cdr. John S. Thach's Fighting Three brought twenty-seven new Grumman F4F-4s, the latest version of the Wildcat. It featured folding wings and six .50-caliber machine guns, instead of four, but only half the ammunition per gun. Fletcher welcomed the increased number of fighters. Pederson, the group commander, thought he was responsible for the shake-up. Earlier in May, not knowing Midway was in the offing, he recommended to Comcarpac that the *Yorktown* squadrons receive a well-earned break. "I told [Noyes] if we were going out to battle I wanted my old air group—that even tho tired and needing a rest they were experienced and used to working together." Noyes refused to relent. Pederson recalled that when Fletcher found out about the new air group, he "was very upset and furious with me for not letting him know of the change. I was really caught in the middle of that one! However, he didn't stay angry too long." As Fletcher told Walter Lord, "It wasn't a question of quality—none could be better—but these new men just weren't used to the ship." Nimitz stuck with the original orders. Events proved that Fletcher and the *Yorktown* would have no cause to complain of their ex-*Saratoga* brethren, far from it.

Ironically the much-improved model of torpedo bomber that all the squadrons long craved finally reached Pearl on 29 May in a convoy from *Alameda* with the Torpedo Eight Detachment (whose parent unit sailed in the *Hornet*) and twenty-one brand new Grumman TBF-1 Avengers. Much faster than the TBDs, the TBFs were also far bigger and heavier. Remarkable for such a big plane (wingspan fifty-four feet, weight 15,905 pounds fully loaded), the Avenger proved an excellent carrier aircraft, long ranged and rugged. As yet only the *Hornet* and the *Saratoga* possessed arresting gear strong enough to take them. Noyes sent six TBFs to Midway in time to fight in the battle. The same stateside convoy also delivered two fresh fighting squadrons, VF-5 (an original *Yorktown* unit) and VF-72, but too late to fight at Midway.

In the brief interval before sailing, Fletcher's staff grappled with a thousand necessary details. Cdr. Hal Guthrie, the combat intelligence and damage control officer, first learned the details of the Midway operation on the morning of 29 May, when he and Cdr. Gerry Galpin, the operations officer, accompanied Fletcher to headquarters. Guthrie followed with obvious interest the progress of the repairs on the *Yorktown*, as her watertight integrity had been compromised, and had serious doubts whether she would survive the next battle. Buckmaster was more sanguine. "The seams were re-riveted, and the bulkheads, doors, and hatches were repaired as best they could in the time they had. My understanding was that it was a patch job, but good enough for us to go to sea, to get into whatever was to happen." . . .

On the morning of 29 May the *Yorktown* left dry dock number one and returned to Pier 16 to resume loading supplies. Work on her innards continued unabated. Nimitz wrote King that she "will be in all respects ready to give a good account of herself." His particularly appropriate postscript evoked the attitude of the entire Pacific Fleet toward fighting at Midway: "We are actively preparing to greet our expected visitors with the kind of reception they deserve, and we will do the best we can with what we have." Bright and early on 30 May Nimitz came on board the *Yorktown* to bid farewell to Fletcher and Buckmaster. He wanted Buckmaster to tell the crew that after the present assignment they were going back to Bremerton for repairs and to enjoy a long leave. For now, however, their task was to help win the biggest battle yet in the Pacific War....

By the time Fletcher sailed, Nimitz had decided on a specific initial position (latitude 32° north, longitude 173° west) 325 miles northeast of Midway to station the carriers while awaiting the enemy approach. He dubbed it "Point Luck." Prior to enemy contact Fletcher was to operate north and east of Luck, Spruance north and west. Toward noon, they were to approach Luck, and, if necessary, communicate by aircraft message drop. Cincpac's dispatch to Spruance called the arrangement "not mandatory" and "intended only to assist initial coordination." The version in Appendix 2 of Op-Plan 29-42 stated that it was "not intended to restrict the operation of either force in any manner but to avoid having embarrassing or premature contact made with own forces." As will be seen, by deliberately not uniting the two task forces Nimitz profoundly shaped how the battle was fought.

On 29 May Cominch provided Nimitz, Fletcher, and Theobald a new estimate of enemy strength and intentions. He now agreed with Nimitz that N-Day, the actual day of the landing, was very likely 5 June. The Midway occupation force apparently left Saipan on 28 May (local time), whereas the Midway Striking Force of the *Akagi*, *Kaga*, *Hiryū*, and *Sōryū* (Cardivs One and Two), four fast battleships, and six heavy cruisers departed Japan the day before. The air attacks on Midway would commence early on 3 June, Midway time. "Believe *Zuikaku* will either form part of the Striking Force or will join convoy as escort on 1 June." King was less certain about the scope and timing of the Aleutians venture with perhaps two small carriers (Cardiv Three), a converted carrier or seaplane tender, and five heavy cruisers, plus screen. The enemy could reach

Kiska on 31 May or 1 June, "Which seems badly timed as effort at diversion." Instead, the carriers might strike Alaska beginning 31 May and 3 June, with an invasion later. "Purpose of attack on date earlier than Midway might be effort at diversion." In fact, as has been seen, the Japanese never intended the AL Operation as a diversion.

On 30 May after TF-17 sailed, Cincpac radioed the task force commanders his latest and most detailed take on the composition of the enemy forces. The Midway Striking Force comprised the familiar four formidable carriers (fortunately not also *Zuikaku*), but its screen numbered only two fast battleships, two heavy cruisers, and a dozen destroyers—a correct estimate. The Midway occupation force should have two or three heavy cruisers, two seaplane carriers, two to four seaplane tenders, twelve to eighteen transports and cargo ships, and a close cover force of one carrier or converted carrier, two fast battleships, five heavy cruisers, and ten destroyers. About sixteen subs preceded the other forces to scout the Hawaii-Midway area. Nimitz's estimate, like King's, failed to include Yamamoto and the battleships of the First Fleet. He also reiterated his belief that the landing at Midway was set for 5 June, a day earlier than the actual Japanese plan. Thus like King, Nimitz estimated the preliminary carrier air attacks could begin the night of 2–3 June. A decrypt revealed a possible rendezvous 685 miles west of Midway, near the extreme strike radius of the B-17s. Given the surmised schedule, that meeting might take place on 31 May or 1 June. Although King speculated that might be where the *Zuikaku* would join the Midway Striking Force, Nimitz labeled it a refueling point. He directed Midway to have B-17s there those two afternoons. They found nothing. No Japanese ships had yet come that far east. Nagumo planned to swing well north before turning southeast toward Midway. The rendezvous itself referred to a later event involving one of Kondō's auxiliaries. Nimitz did not reveal to Fletcher and Spruance that the source of detailed radio intelligence was drying up. The IJN finally implemented the long overdue change with a new cipher codebook and additive table, although some commands used the old system a short while. Thus Hypo and its colleagues in Washington and Melbourne could only analyze radio traffic and break recent messages sent in the old cipher. . . .

On 31 May TF-17 steamed uneventfully northwest toward its fueling rendezvous the next afternoon. Overnight it traversed the waters destined for part of the northern Japanese submarine picket line. Even if those subs had arrived on schedule (1 June, west longitude date), they were too late to detect TF-17. Spruance's TF-16, of course, already lurked far to the northwest. On the morning of 1 June Fletcher's cruisers fueled the destroyers. That day the *Yorktown*'s crew handed out battle gear. To prevent confusion between the two bombing squadrons, Buckmaster temporarily changed Bombing Five's designation to Scouting Five. The weather closed in that afternoon. Twenty minutes after the destroyers finished their drink, the Fueling Group hove into sight. Each cruiser latched onto an oiler. At sundown Fletcher released the *Cimarron* and destroyer *Monssen* to a holding area six to seven hundred miles east of Midway and tucked the *Platte* and *Dewey* astern of TF-17 as it continued west. At dawn on 2 June, as TF-17 closed Point Luck from the southeast, the *Yorktown* took her turn alongside the *Platte*. The skies were overcast, with intermittent patches of misty rain and fog. After the *Yorktown* completed fueling, Fletcher dispatched the oilers to safer waters and headed west toward Point Luck ninety miles off. Although TF-17 sheltered behind Midway's wide-ranging patrol planes, the *Yorktown* mounted a precautionary SBD search. A special flight of two SBDs discovered TF-16 in the midst of clouds sixty miles west of Point Luck and dropped a message to Spruance setting the rendezvous at Luck that afternoon. TF-16 experienced an uneventful trip out. Spruance topped off his ships on 31 May, and from 1 June marked time northeast of Midway, awaiting either Fletcher or the enemy, whoever came first. . . .

Carrier Tactics

On the afternoon of 2 June TF-16 hove into view fifteen miles southwest of TF-17. Unlike the previous month at the Coral Sea, Fletcher did not unite the two task forces, but directed TF-16 to take position ten miles to the south and remain within visual signaling distance. The task forces were to keep five to ten miles apart, with TF-16 holding station to the southwest. Fletcher reluctantly followed Nimitz's direct orders, based on the preference of the top naval aviators for separated carrier task forces. Every reference by Cincpac referred to the task forces as distinct entities. Even the two TF-16 carriers were to maneuver independently under air attack. Fletcher himself much preferred an integrated striking force. In 1947 he told Morison he "automatically assumed command" of the carrier striking force at the rendezvous. "However, due to the lack of time for conferences, drill, preparation of plans and organization," the "clumsy and illogical method was adopted of leaving Spruance in command of his two [carriers], while I retained command of the *Yorktown* Task Force and overall tactical command of the combined force." The two task forces "operated in close vicinity, but not as a tactical unit." Unaware of Cincpac's dictum, critics questioned why Fletcher did not immediately join TF-16 and TF-17, particularly in light of the integral multi-carrier task forces so successful later. Bates incorrectly described Cincpac having organized the carriers "into a single striking force," but did not know why Fletcher failed to incorporate them into the same formation. In truth unlike the Japanese, the U.S. Navy had not yet worked three carriers together, except as George Murray emphasized in November 1942, only "to a very limited extent" and then "*only* for simple, peacetime operations."

Nimitz, however, had his own reasons for not joining the three carriers that went well beyond the worry of employing experimental tactics in battle. He had resolved the contradiction between the Ultra decrypt hinting that carriers would repeatedly strike Midway from very close and the considered belief of his trusted advisor Davis that the carriers would stand well off and refrain from shuttle attacks until they had neutralized Midway's air force. Nimitz now believed the Japanese carriers would do both. The enemy would most likely operate his carriers again in two separate, mutually supporting groups, as it was thought they had repeatedly done before. Separating the carrier groups by at least double the limit of visibility (say fifty miles) prevented a single snooper from spotting both groups. That was the cherished dispersion tactic of the top U.S. naval aviators, but not of Capt. Ted Sherman and Fletcher.

Thus Cincpac Op-Plan 29-42 opined, "One or more carriers may take up close-in daylight positions" to the northwest for up to two days to knock out Midway's air force, while "additional carrier groups and fast battleships" covered these "attacking carriers against our surface forces." Nimitz clearly believed such an initial separation of enemy carriers greatly enhanced his chances for a devastating counterattack, particularly if it came as a complete surprise. The key was to take advantage of surprise to eliminate one enemy carrier group at the outset. The group attacking Midway was likeliest to be spotted first. There was the added benefit of possibly catching its planes on deck being rearmed for further strikes against the island. The primary weapon for this attack was to be Spruance's TF-16 (*Enterprise* and *Hornet*), kept "cocked and primed" as a single unit, while other forces handled searches. Once one Japanese carrier group appeared within range, Fletcher, wielding tactical command, would instantly release Spruance to hurl his full striking power of 120 planes, capable of destroying at least two carriers at once. Browning's staff was to ensure this supremely vital attack went off without a hitch. In the meantime, Fletcher would decide whether TF-17 (*Yorktown*) engaged the second enemy group—the most desirable course of action—or followed up Spruance's attack. Fletcher retained the flexibility to launch searches and fill in with attacks against one group or the other as necessary. Should events go the way Nimitz, Fletcher, and Spruance hoped, the second phase would see three U.S. carriers finish off the two remaining flattops. In truth, Nagumo never divided his four carriers. That misunderstanding on the part of Nimitz and others would cause grave repercussions in the subsequent battle. . . .

On the afternoon of 2 June Fletcher followed Cincpac's suggestion to move north of Midway, rather than keep to the northeast. The two task forces headed west at fourteen knots during the night to gain proper position, should, as expected, the Japanese carriers show up at dawn on 3 June northwest of Midway. If the enemy was delayed, Fletcher planned to work northward during most of the day and then retire southward toward Midway to avoid running afoul of a possible surface force approaching in the darkness. Anticipation in both task forces ran high. "Morale was excellent."

9 "ILLUSTRATIVE BATTLES"

(Selection from chapter 12 of *A History of Naval Tactical Thought*)

Admiral of the Fleet Giuseppe Fioravanzo, Italian Navy

The two most influential books I read when trying to understand modern tactics were Robison's *History of Naval Tactics from 1530 to 1930* and Fioravanzo's *History of Naval Tactical Thought*. Both books, though comprehensive, failed to deliver the substance of modern tactics in the present missile era, or the fast-approaching era of robots. They were written too long ago. But they taught me to look for what changed over the years and why. For example, the present missile era though mature in time has only had a limited number of combat examples to guide tactical thinking.

Fioravanzo's *History* is rich both in describing tactical essentials and in illustrating progressive developments with examples through the carrier era of World War II. His emphasis is on ways to achieve superior concentration of combat power and on the advantages of striking first.

To illustrate, from Chapter 12 I have selected the decisive Battle of the Yalu in the Sino-Japanese War of 1894–95. The extract describes in analytical and diagrammatic detail the tactics that won the battle for Japan. It reflects a fierce debate over the advantages of a column or a "V"-formation of ships steaming nearly abreast. In turn, the choice of formation rested on faith in the gun or in armor. A line abreast was better for ramming when armor was ascendant, but a column was better for concentrating gunfire. The battle was the first action between two fleets in motion since the Battle of Lissa in 1866, when ramming returned to prominence for the first time since galley warfare. The latter half of the nineteenth century was a time when armor was strong enough to be a dominant consideration, analogous to the trust we confided in surface-to-air missiles (SAMs) to defeat Soviet bombers and missiles in the 1970s. In both instances the "defender advantage" had not been tested in a fleet battle for many years. Our SAMs have never been tested against a saturating missile attack.

Battleship tactics are obsolete, but they are reminders of the phenomenal change that occurred with the arrival of the aircraft carrier era. In World War II, maneuvers by ships shifted to maneuvers by much faster aircraft. Then thirty years later, ballistic and cruise missiles arrived with their own form of "maneuvers," demanding new ways of understanding the tactical offense/defense relationship. Early placement of ships in a formation or disposition has increased in importance, because in the missile era the *lethal phase* of the battle will start and end before the ships can change formation.

What will be the effect of autonomous vehicles? This is hard to anticipate, but experiments being done at the Naval Postgraduate School and elsewhere show that swarms of mutually cooperating aerial vehicles are just over the horizon. It will be interesting to see how we teach (program into) these swarming autonomous vehicles their own winning tactics!

"ILLUSTRATIVE BATTLES"

(Selection from chapter 12 of *A History of Naval Tactical Thought*) by
Admiral of the Fleet Giuseppe Fioravanzo, Italian Navy (Naval Institute Press,
1959): 146–48.

Battle of the Yalu

This battle was the only one fought on the open sea during the Chino-Japanese
War (June 1894–April 1895), in which sea power, nevertheless, played a determining role because both belligerents had to use the sea since they had no common
frontiers.

The battle took place on 25 September 1894, when the Japanese squadron
(Admiral Ito, with his second in command, Admiral Tsuboi) encountered the
Chinese squadron (Admiral Ting) off the mouth of the Yalu River, as it was
returning to Port Arthur after escorting a convoy of troops that disembarked in
the vicinity of that river.

The opposing naval forces were:

Chinese: two 7,300-ton armorclads with a speed of 14 knots and main
weapons consisting of four 305-mm. guns in two turrets positioned obliquely;
two 3,000-ton cruisers with a speed of 16 knots and mounting 254-mm. guns,
with the area of maximum concentration of gunfire ahead; two 2,500-ton,
15-knot cruisers mounting 230-mm. guns; six protected cruisers between 1,000
and 2,000 tons. In all, twelve units, ten of which participated in the action.

Japanese: three 4,000-ton armorclads with a speed of 14 knots and having
as main weapons four single 240-mm. guns, two on a side; three 2,500-ton,
17-knot protected cruisers mounting one 320mm. gun en barbette at the bow
and some 120-mm. guns; two 2,200-ton, 16-knot protected cruisers mounting 254-mm. and 152-mm. guns; two smaller, more modern 16-knot protected
cruisers, mounting 152s and 120s. Attached to the squadron were one gunboat
and one transport, which did not participate in the battle.

At the beginning of the action the deployment of the units of the two
adversaries was as shown in Figure 38.

Figure 38: The Approach

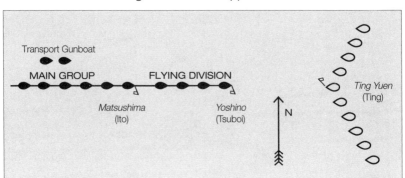

Ito had regrouped his forces into a single column, in two divisions: one, at the head, under the command of Tsuboi, composed of the four swiftest units; the other in the rear, commanded by Ito himself, composed of the remaining ships, of which the three armorclads were the slowest. At the side, toward the rear, were the gunboat and the transport.

Ting had deployed his ten ships in wedge formation with the two battleships in the center and the rest four on each side, distributed without any idea of homogeneity.

On the whole, the Chinese squadron was more powerfully armed and better protected; the eight 305s of the two armorclads were sufficient to establish superiority. The Japanese squadron had a larger number of fast ships.

Victory smiled on the Japanese because Ito, taking advantage of superior speed, maneuvered skillfully and used vigorously all the firepower at his disposal, while Ting, restricted to the unwieldy wedge, was either unable or unwilling to countermaneuver or to take full advantage of his heavy firepower.

In the final analysis, this battle represented the triumph of mobility in support of gunfire, against sluggish maneuvering with consequent dearth of gunfire. The employment of the ram was not possible and was not even attempted, because the one who might have used it was slower than his adversary.

The action is shown in Figure 39. The figures indicate the corresponding positions of the two antagonists:

1— Initial positions when the opening of fire was imminent (about 1230 hours).

2— Ito makes for the Chinese right wing, attacking with heavy raking fire.

3— The Chinese between two fires, Tsuboi having turned to protect the gunboat and the transport which had opened distance.

4— The Japanese dual action on both sides of the wedge continues.

5— The Chinese formation, split into two groups by the loss of three vessels (two on the right wing and one on the left), finally gives way and attempts to withdraw from the action (around 1530 hours).

Figure 39: The Battle Manuevers

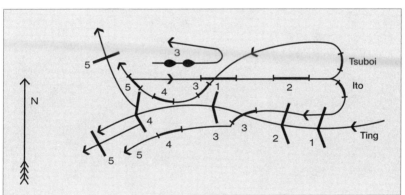

At 1530, the Chinese squadron was in a predicament: in addition to the three ships lost, two others were seriously damaged and had been forced to leave the arena. The five surviving ships had also sustained some damage and were short of ammunition. The heavy but disordered Chinese fire had caused much less damage to the Japanese ships.

After reorganizing the formation and having placed his ship at the head, Ito set out to resume the battle, but a heavy-caliber shot damaged Ito's ship, and she was forced to leave formation. Without the Admiral acting as guide, the squadron performed sluggishly, in spite of Ito's signals. After the squadron was reorganized for the second time, two hours later (that is, at about 1730) Ito resumed pursuit of Ting's surviving vessels, but the appearance of some Chinese torpedo boats and the imminence of nightfall discouraged him from persisting. The next clay, Ito continued to seek the enemy on the way to Weihaiwei, but the enemy ships had safely reached Port Arthur.

Thus ended a battle which could have resulted in the destruction of the entire Chinese squadron if it had been waged vigorously to the very end. Later, locked in Weihaiwei, the Chinese squadron was completely destroyed by the same Admiral Ito's persistent attacks on the fortress and torpedo boat attacks within the anchorage.

10 "CREATING ASW KILLING ZONES"

LCDR James Stavridis, USN

Most of my career was devoted to antisubmarine warfare. Several sea tours were in ASW hunter-killer groups, in destroyers screening task forces or critical shipping, or in shore assignments that designed campaign plans similar to those described by Jim Stavridis, then a lieutenant commander. By the late 1980s the U.S. Navy's campaign plan to defend against Soviet submarines and threaten attacks on Soviet SSBNs had become stylized, if not stultified. Stavridis decries the danger of ignoring enemy choices and proposes a more flexible Navy campaign plan that will adapt to unexpected Soviet deployments.

We may all be grateful that our strategy for a NATO war was never put to the test. Now we must shape flexible plans for new prospective enemies around the world, with new technologies that include unmanned underwater systems. Now, more than twenty-five years after he wrote his essay, Stavridis' advice is again pertinent for the rise of China and the resurgence of Russia.

It is a pleasure to include Admiral Stavridis' early essay, because it demonstrates that a thoughtful young writer can rise to the top of his profession, contrary to what some of my seniors told me, which was "don't get too far out in front by proposing original ideas." Until

2009 he was one of the U.S. Navy's most influential leaders, truly a "soldier-scholar," who commanded ships, fleets, and theaters to good effect. Currently Dr. Stavridis is dean of the Fletcher School of Law and Diplomacy at Tufts University and chairman of the board of the U.S. Naval Institute.

"CREATING ASW KILLING ZONES"

By LCDR James Stavridis, USN, U.S. Naval Institute *Proceedings* (October 1987): 38–42.

If we think of the Northern Hemisphere as a large target composed of three killing zones, the bull's-eye will cover the Soviet submarine bastions around the North Pole.

One of the key determinants of the Navy's ability to execute the Maritime Strategy will be the tactical and strategic efficiency of antisubmarine warfare (ASW) efforts. The Secretary of the Navy, the Chief of Naval Operations, and numerous flag officers all have pointed to ASW as a top priority in all warfighting operations. An unfolding and variable Soviet submarine strategy may require a combination of barrier operations against nuclear-powered attack submarines (SSNs) and nuclear-powered guided-missile submarines (SSGNs) and highly offensive ASW campaigns against nuclear-powered fleet ballistic submarines (SSBNs). The effective execution of ASW tactics and strategy will require a high degree of interoperability among sensors and weapon systems. One way to do this will be to establish a set of killing zones in areas where Soviet submarines are likely to be concentrated and to assign coordinated packages of sensors and weapon systems to each zone. One key addition to current ASW forces will be squadrons built around new surface ships that can act as linebackers and mobile attack groups in the ASW battle. With proper timing, ASW efforts can be directed through the killing zones in sequential waves, permitting mutual support, enhancing kill opportunity and accomplishment, and ensuring a minimal level of either interference or costly blue-on-blue engagements (i.e., encounters with friendly forces) in the high-tempo operations that the Maritime Strategy envisions. Essentially, both tactical and strategic ASW will need to be executed as part of a coordinated ASW battle.

The Role of ASW in the Maritime Strategy: The basic outline of the Maritime Strategy has been well-publicized by now. In Phase I—*Deterrence/Transition to War*—major blocks of U.S. forces, especially ASW platforms, will deploy forward into attack positions. In Phase II—*Seizing the Initiative*—sea control will be established in forward zones. Finally, Phase III—*Carrying the Fight to the Enemy*—includes projection of power against the Soviet homeland.

ASW will be the most difficult task in the strategy's execution. In the unclassified description of the strategy published as a supplement to the Naval Institute *Proceedings* in January 1986, ASW operations in Phase I are described generally as a process by which "aggressive forward movement of ASW forces, both submarines and maritime patrol aircraft, will force Soviet submarines to retreat into defensive bastions to protect their ballistic missile submarines." In Phase II, "It will be essential to conduct forward operations with attack submarines, as well as to establish barriers at key world choke points using maritime patrol aircraft, mines, attack submarines, or sonobuoys, to prevent leakage of enemy forces to the open ocean where the Western Alliance's resupply lines can be threatened." Finally, Phase III indicates that "antisubmarine warfare forces would continue to destroy Soviet submarines, including ballistic missile submarines, thus reducing the attractiveness of nuclear escalation by changing the nuclear balance in our favor."

Most analysts believe that the Soviet SSNs and SSBNs will probably withdraw together into bastions under the ice near the Soviet homeland, and that the top NATO priority will then become finding and killing them. As one observer recently pointed out in *Proceedings*, "U.S. ASW forces will need to expedite their campaign against Soviet SSBNs. Altering the nuclear balance by destroying submarines is a chief source of war termination leverage. Other ASW missions should remain a lower priority."

All of this is sound—if risky—strategy. Beyond the risks of executing the basic anti-SSBN strategy is the unpredictability of Soviet response to the potential loss of their SSBN deterrent. Simply put, the Soviets may not follow the plan outlined above. War is uncertainty. The Soviets may indeed take a conservative approach and withdraw assets under the ice close to their homeland. On the other hand, they may choose to rely to a great degree on their other strategic forces and use their submarines (notably their SSNs and SSGNs) very differently. A few Soviet alternatives include the following:

> ➤ Send their SSBNs farther into open waters with one to two SSNs or SSGNs in a shotgun role. This would free the SSNs to break off momentarily and attack allied warships or commercial shipping. The Soviets have more than 60 modern SSBNs and roughly 120 SSNs and SSGNs—enough to allow them to execute such a strategy easily. Because of the flexibility of putting SSNs and SSGNs in forward positions, they could use these submarines in both an offensive (against carrier battle groups [CVBGs] and allied sea lines of communication [SLOCs]) and a defensive (pro-SSBN) role. Naturally, this would entail a higher degree of risk to their SSBNs, at least until more and quieter Typhoons appear with the newer SSNs and SSGNs. If the new Akula-class submarines are as formidable as many observers think, such a strategy may be attractive to the Soviets because it would effectively set up traps against the U.S. SSNs pursuing their SSBNs.

> ➤ Leave SSBNs in bastions, but defend them with a minimal number of SSNs and rely principally upon other means to protect them (such as the improving Soviet ASW air and surface forces). This would free up a number of SSNs to attack allied warships or commercial shipping.

> ➤ Send SSGNs to sea in land-attack roles against peripheral U.S. and allied installations and bases in key locations—Subic Bay, Rota, Holy Loch, and Diego Garcia.

> ➤ Attempt to limit any conflict to strictly conventional weapons and send all SSNs and SSGNs into open waters in a classic antishipping

campaign, as did Germany in both world wars. The Soviets could then threaten vertical escalation if the United States undertook strikes against their SSBNs.

➤ Wage an anti-choke point campaign with a limited number of SSGNs and SSNs, while still leaving significant forces behind in a "shotgun" role. This might offer the Soviets the most "bang for the buck."

➤ Execute some combination of the above strategies—dividing the forces either by time, geography, or mission.

The only certainty is that the Soviet strategy will be variable and unpredictable. The key for U.S. ASW forces will be flexibility, offensive punch, and coordination. ASW operations will be intrinsically tied to the national strategy as the war escalates—more so than any other warfare area. This is because of the obvious linkages between the fate of Soviet strategic assets (their SSBNs) and the basic conflict. If the war continues to escalate, and, for example, encompasses the sinking of many Soviet SSBNs, the Soviets will be faced with very difficult and dangerous decisions. Our ASW efforts must be carefully tied to the Soviet strategy and to our own national policy goals.

Killing Zones: Given the opening argument that the Soviet submarine strategy will not remain predictable, U.S. forces must establish an offensive frame of mind and a geographic reference system for flexible attack options. The point, of course, is that the Maritime Strategy must be prepared to respond to a variety of scenarios. It might be helpful to establish a set of geographically defined ASW areas and to prioritize the application of sensors, weapon systems, and general forces in each.

➤ *Red Zone:* If the Soviets opt for a classic bastion strategy, these critical areas will probably contain the Soviet SSBNs, primarily the longer-range intercontinental ballistic missile (ICBM)-equipped Delta and Typhoon classes. They will be located in the protected regional waters near the Soviet Union, including the under-ice and open areas of the

Arctic Ocean, the White Sea, the Barents Sea, the Kara Sea, the Laptev Sea, the East Siberian Sea, and the Sea of Okhotsk.

➤ *Orange Zone:* In the bastion strategy, Soviet SSNs would probably operate in the Orange Zone in a barrier operation to protect the entrances to Red Zone bastions and to destroy any U.S. strike forces (CVBG or Tomahawk battleship, guided-missile cruiser, or destroyer strike groups) seeking to close on the Soviet Union. These areas include the Sea of Japan, the Bering Sea, the waters north of the Greenland-Iceland-United Kingdom Gap, and the Beaufort Sea.

➤ *Yellow Zone:* Soviet SSNs and SSGNs operating in the Yellow Zone would be able to attack allied SLOCs. The Yellow Zone might comprise the Northern Pacific, including sea lanes between the United States and Japan; the Northern Atlantic, including the vital SLOCs between the United States and Europe; the Indian Ocean; and the South China Sea. In addition, Soviet SSNs could attack allied warships and commercial shipping in the Mediterranean, the Baltic, and other ASW theaters. Soviet SSGNs may also operate here in a land-attack role against peripheral U.S. installations.

In each of the zones, U.S. ASW forces would be keyed to proceed and commence attacking Soviet submarine forces, as necessary, given the overall war situations. By keying operations to such zones, ASW efforts can be better coordinated as follows:

➤ To reduce or eliminate blue-on-blue engagements, large geographic areas can be established as keep-out zones for certain classes of U.S. ASW forces. Red Zones, for example, could be assigned to SSBNs, Orange to long-range maritime patrol aircraft (LRMP), and Yellow to CVBG/ASW squadrons. In addition, allied ASW forces could be assigned certain portions of various zones.

➤ Timing decisions could be keyed to the geographic areas. For example, U.S. SSNs could sweep the Yellow and Orange Zones on their way to the free-fire Red Zone. Contacts in prosecution can be turned over to LRMP or surface forces as necessary.

➤ ASW Operations Centers (ASWOCs) could manage contacts through the zones, ensuring more efficient placement of sensors and weapons on targets.

➤ In the event of command-and-control problems, preplanned responses, as required by time or in response to Soviet action, could be tied to the zones.

➤ Individual units could be assigned to train and operate in each geographic area during peacetime to allow for greater in-area expertise.

Coordinated Operations: The real key to executing the ASW portion of the Maritime Strategy will be coordination through the killing zones by very disparate forces. This coordination will be based on critical timing decisions. All of the actions will be tied to the Maritime Strategy. One possible time line, which illustrates this complexity and is written to respond to an initial Soviet bastion strategy followed by an open ocean break, might appear as follows:

Phase I: *Transition to War:*

➤ U.S. SSNs sweep through Yellow and Orange zones, and proceed to the Red Zone.

➤ Sonar surveillance system (SOSUS) stations are keyed.

➤ SSN contacts in Orange Zone are turned over to LRMP.

➤ ASW squadrons (*Ticonderoga* [CG-47]-class guided-missile cruisers for antiair warfare, two *Spruance* [DD-963]-class destroyers with LAMPS Mk III and sonar towed arrays, and two *Oliver Hazard Perry* [FFG-7]-class guided-missile frigates with LAMPS Mk III and sonar tails move into linebacker station at edge of Orange Zone.

➤ CVBG (if available) prepares to move into Yellow Zones as required for strikes in larger conflict. If assets are available, prepare strikes at SSN and SSBN bases.

> Mobile logistics support force (MLSF) 'with all possible torpedoes' moves to edge of Yellow Zone to perform delivery-boy services to ASW squadrons and CVBGs.

Phase II: *Seize the Initiative:*

> Assess Soviet plan for use of their SSNs and SSBNs. (This is probably the key step in the process.)
> Make national-level decisions concerning kill/no kill of Soviet SSBNs in bastions or elsewhere.
> If strategy is antibastion, U.S. SSNs begin killing Soviet subs in the Red Zone.
> LRMPs begin killing in Orange Zones.
> ASW squadrons establish barriers at edges of Orange and Yellow Zones and kill all contacts.
> CVBGs move to positions as required for strikes against SSBN bases (Kola, Petrovskiy, Vladivostok) and submarine-capable shipyards and docks (Severodvinsk in the Arctic, Admiralty in the Baltic, Sudomeh in the Baltic, and Komosomolsk in the Pacific). Ensure that strikes eliminate all Soviet submarine bases and sources of SSN and SSBN support.
> MLSF undertakes resupply of ASW forces, as required.

Phase III: *Carrying the Fight to the Enemy:*

> Reassess Soviet plan, which may have changed, based on events in Phase II, to include open ocean warfighting.
> Continue SSN campaigns in forward areas or pull back to cleared sectors in the Orange Zones.
> Shift LRMP forces into linebacker role with ASW squadrons to await possible open-ocean break of Soviet SSNs.
> Station CVBG to respond to tasking of war termination.
> ASW squadrons launch coordinated geographic operations with remaining LRMP to establish barriers.
> MLSF await resupply operations.

ASW Squadrons: As indicated, ASW squadrons can undertake many key line-backer missions. This is a concept the United States has flirted with for many years. An excellent mix of ships is currently available for such a mission, including the *Spruance* class, some of which are being converted to operate the superb LAMPS Mk III ASW helicopter; the *Oliver Perry Hazard* class, most of which are LAMPS Mk III-capable; and the *Ticonderoga* class, which offers excellent ASW and good AAW protection in low-medium air threat areas. The major advantages of standing up four compact ASW squadrons of four to five ships each include:

- Better results by training in an essentially single warfare area
- Excellent coordination and teamwork from repeated team ASW operations (ASW is a team sport.)
- Carefully selected mix of complementary weapons and sensors
- Expertise in the complexities of modern ASW at the deckplate level
- Multi-mission group that could undertake barrier operations, offensive hunter-killer tactics, shifts to convoy protection, and even pro-U.S. SSBN operations, if new Soviet (Akula-class, for example) SSNs moved to attack U.S. boats

Conclusions and Recommendations: All ASW warfighting must be coordinated by ASWOCs working under fleet commanders, who have the connections to the national level decision-making arena that will be required to execute the sensitive anti-SSBN strategic portions of the strategy. The difficulty will lie in assessing Soviet submarine strategy, which will change depending on the direction of the war, the objectives, and the decision-making process in the Kremlin.

Ultimately, ASW in support of the Maritime Strategy will require a high degree of flexibility, coordinated operations, and timing across a wide range of geographic areas. Further study of ASW operations in the Maritime Strategy must be undertaken. As a starting point:

- Examine more possible Soviet submarine options and strategies. Much of our current planning is fixed on the notion that the Soviets will automatically withdraw their SSBNs into bastions and protect them with virtually their entire SSN force. This might not be the case. The Maritime Strategy must be prepared to meet more options.

- Conduct major ocean coordinated ASW exercises to examine various tactical and strategic mixes of all of our ASW forces. Train to respond to a variety of Soviet submarine strategic approaches. Work to improve the interoperability among U.S. and allied ASW forces.

- Continue to develop ASW squadrons as CVBG and battleship surface-action-group force requirements permit. Mission training should be very flexible and should include open-ocean ASW, barrier operations, large-scale coordinated operations with LRMP and SSNs, and pro-U.S. SSBN operations.

- Implement Red-Orange-Yellow Zone as a method for geographic reference in the Maritime Strategy.

ASW will be the major challenge in the Maritime Strategy. It will demand the best in all the coordinated arms of the Navy to execute a wide variety of potential ASW plans against a massive and unpredictable Soviet submarine force.

11 "A POOR MAN'S NAVAL DEFENSE" AND "ANTI-LANDING DEFENSE AND THE IMPLICATIONS FOR FUTURE AMPHIBIOUS OPERATIONS"

(Selections from chapters 11 and 13 of *At the Water's Edge*)

Theodore L. Gatchel

Ted Gatchel takes his inspiration from Sir Walter Raleigh, who said, "It is more difficult to defend a coast than to invade it." Sir Walter may have been thinking of the many Norse and Saxon invasions of Britain, and the Norman Conquest of 1066. Gatchel emphasizes the problems of the defender 850 years later, from World War II through the successful United Kingdom campaign to take back the Falklands from Argentina. He shows that no well-equipped and well-trained amphibious assault force has ever failed to get ashore. True, some of the landings have been near-run things, and many have been bloody affairs for both sides, but Gatchel's aim is to show how an attacker has successfully exploited defender disadvantages in the past.

My first selection from his book describes the very high risk amphibious assault at Inchon in September 1950. The physical hazards at the port looked impossible to overcome, so much so as to create complacency in the North Korean defenders who occupied Seoul. Our attack succeeded because we had a residue of experienced amphibious leaders from World War II and enough experienced forces to mount the assault. The reward was enormous, for the successful landing broke the spirit of the overextended North Korean forces, liberated South

Korea, and was totally successful in driving the invaders back into the north. My second selection is Gatchel's recapitulation of historical defender disadvantages, some natural, some self-induced. These he places side by side with what it took for an expeditionary force to succeed. It has been twenty years since Gatchel wrote, and even longer since the Royal Navy retook the Falklands in 1982 in the last opposed assault. Things that have not changed since 1982 are the severe hazards and the vastness of the maritime battle space compared to a ground campaign. Again we see that the operational and tactical levels of a modern campaign at sea are virtually indistinguishable.

Colonel Gatchel emphasizes the tactics of expeditionary operations, but he starts his book with some astute comments on the strategic advantages of a maritime power. These advantages are broader than Mahan's emphasis on command of the seas, the importance of trade, and the role of capital ships to achieve a decisive battle. He quotes Raleigh again: "And I know it to be true that a fleet of ships may be seen at sunset, and after it at the Lizard, yet by the next morning they may recover Portland; whereas an army on foot shall not be able to march it in six dayes." Raleigh does not exaggerate. For a thousand years an army transported at sea has moved an order of magnitude faster than an army on the land. A long-standing rule of thumb is that an unopposed ground force moves about twenty-five miles a day. In our successful blitzkrieg during Operation Iraqi Freedom, Army and Marine forces averaged twenty miles a day to topple the Saddam Hussein regime in just three weeks and a day. Yet that "swift" movement is incomparably slower than a force transported by sea. Gatchel sums up a sea power's advantage this way: "In spite of the availability of modern ground and air transportation to defenders today, navies continue to maintain their traditional mobility advantage . . . no army can move with enough combat power to repulse a major assault before the landing force has established itself ashore."

"A POOR MAN'S NAVAL DEFENSE" AND "ANTI-LANDING DEFENSE AND THE IMPLICATIONS FOR FUTURE AMPHIBIOUS OPERATIONS"

(Selections from chapters 11 and 13 of *At the Water's Edge*) by Theodore L. Gatchel (Naval Institute Press, 1996): 175–77 and 203–17.

The Situation at Inchon

Geography alone made Inchon an unlikely target for an amphibious assault. The greatest advantages that the North Koreans possessed there had been created by the forces of nature. Inchon's tidal range of more than thirty-two feet is one of the world's greatest. The harbor itself must be approached by one of two narrow channels swept by rapid currents. Easily blocked by mines, the channels were potential death traps for a fleet of amphibious ships. In addition, Inchon had no landing beaches in the conventional sense. At high tide, the invaders would encounter stone seawalls along the port's waterfront. Low tide, on the other hand, exposed a mud flat that was two miles wide in places and impassible by vehicles or troops on foot. To make matters even worse, the seawalls that would have to serve as beaches were dominated by Wolmi-do, a small island in the harbor that was connected to the mainland by a causeway.

Determined to destroy the enemy pocket at Pusan, the North Koreans appear to have given little thought to defending Inchon against an amphibious assault. In the vicinity of Seoul, the NKPA had approximately 44,000 troops consisting of the 18th Rifle Division and a large number of independent units. Approximately 2,200 troops from the 226th Marine Regiment and elements of the 918th (Coast) Artillery Regiment defended Inchon. The 400 troops on Wolmi-do had emplaced Soviet 76-mm guns in bunkers overlooking the harbor. In the five years since the end of World War II, the Americans had failed to gather even basic information about the conditions at Inchon. In an effort to correct this oversight, Lt. Eugene F. Clark, USN, and a small group of Americans and Koreans landed on the nearby island of Yonghung-do on 1 September.

Working with local guerrillas, Lieutenant Clark's group gathered badly needed intelligence about Inchon's tides and beaches.

As the landing force for his amphibious end run, General MacArthur selected the U.S. X Corps, under command of Maj. Gen. Edward M. Almond, who had been MacArthur's chief of staff in Tokyo when he received the Korean assignment. Two divisions would make up X Corps for the landing. The 1st Marine Division, minus one of its own regiments but reinforced by a regiment of ROK Marines, would conduct the assault. The division's third regiment would join up as soon as it arrived from the United States. The U.S. Army's 7th Infantry Division would land after the Marines as a follow-on force. Total strength, including ROK reinforcements and Marine Corps aviation units, was just over 71,000 troops. Compared with North Korean units at Inchon and Seoul, X Corps was not an overwhelming force.

A bigger problem for MacArthur, however, was assembling the naval forces needed to conduct a division-size amphibious assault. Although the British contributed two cruisers to the naval gunfire support group, the task of transporting the troops fell largely to the U.S. Navy. In the five years since the end of World War II, the U.S. Navy had dismantled what had been the greatest amphibious fleet ever assembled. The state of the navy's amphibious force in 1950 is illustrated by the problems of Rear Adm. James H. Doyle, commander of Amphibious Group One, in obtaining a minimum of forty-seven LSTs to carry out the plan. Unfortunately, the navy that had employed more than two hundred LSTs for the invasion of Okinawa in 1945 could muster only seventeen in time for the landing at Inchon. MacArthur solved Doyle's problems by recalling thirty LSTs that the United States had given the Japanese government after World War II to use in coastal trade. The ships were in bad condition and had Japanese crews, many of whom were former members of the Imperial Japanese Navy. U.S. Marines thus had the strange experience of being carried to war by their previous enemies.

In developing his landing plan, Maj. Gen. Oliver P. Smith, commanding general of the 1st Marine Division, insisted on seizing Wolmi-do before landing in the city of Inchon. This meant that, if the Marines were to land on Wolmi-do on the morning high tide, they would have to wait until 1700 before the tide was again high enough for the main landing at Inchon. Because the ebbing tide would then leave the Marines stranded in Inchon without the possibility of being resupplied until the next morning, Marine logisticians conceived a daring plan. As soon as the Marines had seized a beachhead at Inchon, the navy would beach eight LSTs, each loaded with five hundred tons of equipment and supplies. Because the tide would recede before the LSTs could be unloaded, they would remain beached on the mud flats overnight. Filled with fuel and explosives, the stranded ships would be sitting ducks for enemy gunners, but no alternatives were available.

Having assembled an adequate amphibious force, MacArthur faced another enemy: time. Beaching the LSTs over Inchon's mud flats required a high tide of at least twenty nine feet. The next tide at that depth would occur on 15 September. If the Americans missed that date, they would have to wait until the middle of October, too long to help relieve the pressure on the Eighth Army. The need for speed dictated that D-day at Inchon be 15 September. . . .

Anti-Landing Defense and the Implications for Future Amphibious Operations

It is more difficult to defend a coast than to invade it.—Sir Walter Raleigh

Since the beginning of modern amphibious warfare at Gallipoli, defenders have searched for a way to defeat a landing. With the exception of three small Japanese landings during World War II, the defenders have been unsuccessful. During this search, defenders have tried virtually all of the possible approaches to anti-landing defense. In the estimates of the attackers, all of the basic approaches have come close to succeeding on occasion. The fierce Japanese defense at the water's edge at Tarawa made the outcome of that landing uncertain during most of D-day. The same can be said of the German water's edge defense on Omaha Beach at Normandy. The German mobile defense at Salerno forced U.S. Gen. Mark W. Clark to consider evacuating the Americans from the beaches. Japanese attempts at naval defense at Guadalcanal, Leyte Gulf, and Okinawa clearly demonstrate the potential of that approach. In spite of these close calls, no major anti-landing defense has ever succeeded.

Sketching the characteristics of an anti-landing defense that would have the greatest chance of succeeding is not difficult. Such a scheme would commence with a naval defense combining the following actions:

- more extensive version of the minefields employed by the North Koreans at Wonsan
- all-out aerial assault against the invasion fleet that is patterned after the Japanese defense of Okinawa, with "smart" weapons replacing the kamikazes
- coordinated D-day attack on the naval forces conducting the landing by midget submarines, fast-attack craft, assault swimmers, and other special units, such as those envisioned but never employed by the Germans at Normandy
- naval attack by major fleet units against the ships carrying and supporting the landing force, such as the operation attempted by the Japanese fleet at Leyte Gulf

The naval defense would be backed up by a defense at the water's edge, which combines the most lethal aspects of the Japanese defense at Tarawa and the German defense at Normandy. Once an enemy landing force had committed itself to assault one of these beaches, it would be counterattacked by heavy armored forces like those that nearly succeeded during the German mobile defense at Salerno. This defense would also include a counterlanding from the sea by specially trained amphibious forces along the lines that the Japanese planned several times during World War II but were never able to carry out.

The entire defense would be coordinated by a single individual who commanded all air, land, and naval forces committed to the defense from a headquarters near the scene of the action. This single commander would have the authority to make any decision needed to implement the defense except the use of chemical or nuclear weapons.

The ease of outlining this defense raises the obvious question of why no one has ever fielded such a defense. One answer might be that it requires a greater commitment of resources than most nations are willing to provide, particularly in peacetime. Historically, even where a defender has made the effort to construct impressive anti-landing defenses—the Atlantic Wall, for example—the amphibious attacker has nevertheless prevailed. Common to many of the failed attempts to defeat a landing are a number of factors that help to explain the overall failure of this particular operation of war. The steps that a potential defender might take to correct these past shortcomings also have important implications for the future of amphibious operations.

The Naval Character of Amphibious Operations

The basic requirement for a successful anti-landing defense is the recognition that an amphibious operation is a naval operation. As obvious as that conclusion is to some military planners, it appears to have escaped most of the commanders who have attempted to defend against landings. Commanders of ground troops participating in a landing are forced to accept the naval character of the operation by the very circumstances in which they find themselves. An amphibious assault requires both navy officers and ground officers to cooperate fully and to recognize the capabilities and limitations of the others' services. The navy must transport the landing force to the invasion site, sometimes against opposition, and deliver the troops to the shore. The landing force contributes little to the operation until it has reached the beach and can commence fighting.

Defending commanders face a quite different set of circumstances. They can act, and frequently have, as if defending against an amphibious operation were simply an operation of ground warfare not unlike the defense of a river line. In many cases, defending army commanders have treated their own naval forces as auxiliaries, rather than as one of the principal means of defeating a landing. General Senger und Etterlin attributed German anti-landing failures during World War II, in part, to the army's failure to understand the naval dimension of modern warfare. In his view, this weakness in the Germans' military thinking consistently caused them to overestimate the ease with which they could either prevent a landing or throw an invasion force back into the sea. Admiral Ruge, in echoing this view, commented on its universal application and noted that naval officers appear to be able to apply their thinking to the land battle easier than army officers can do the reverse.

Other German officers have taken issue with this view, but the record of World War II seems to support Senger und Etterlin's thesis. The Japanese, on the other hand, fully understood the naval character of amphibious warfare, yet they could never bring themselves to act resolutely on that understanding with respect to defending against Allied landings. Instead, they chose to give precedence to forcing a decisive naval engagement with the U.S. fleet.

The danger for the U.S. military today is that it will lose sight of the essential naval character of amphibious operations. Emphasis is overwhelmingly focused on joint operations, with the result that single-service capabilities are not always fully appreciated. In spite of this emphasis on "jointness," an amphibious operation remains primarily a naval operation, even when forces from the army and air force participate. Perhaps the distinction seems academic, but it is an important one.

Command Relationships

The very nature of an amphibious operation requires ground and naval commanders to acknowledge one another's participation in the enterprise and demands a minimum level of cooperation. Because the navy must carry the landing force to the objective area and deliver it to a beach from which it can carry out its mission ashore, navy planners must at least consider the landing force's needs when planning the navy's part in the operation. The basic nature of a defense against a landing, on the other hand, exerts no corresponding pressure on commanders from different services to cooperate or consider the requirements of the other services. In many cases, naval and ground commanders defending against an enemy landing virtually have acted independently of one another.

This difference between conducting a landing and defending against one works to the advantage of the amphibious attacker by increasing the chances that the attacker's plan will reflect both unity of command and unity of effort.

Defenders are not precluded from achieving such unity, but the nature of anti-landing defense does not demand it the way an amphibious operation does.

Historically, landings have been commanded at the operational level by admirals and defended against by generals. Notable exceptions to this rule were the Japanese island defenses in the Gilberts and Marshalls, which were commanded by admirals. Formal command relationships between commanders conducting landings have usually followed one of two patterns. Most of the central Pacific landings in World War II were conducted with command of all air, sea, and land forces in the hands of a naval officer who commanded a numbered fleet. Command relationships in the European landings, on the other hand, were generally based on the British concept of cooperation. Even then, the naval commanders normally exercised control over the landing force until the situation ashore reached the point where ground commanders could take control of the operation. Unlike those in the Pacific, however, air commanders in European operations refused to place their forces under naval command.

Given the record since Gallipoli, one salient lesson stands out. At the operational level, command of a defense against an expected landing should be placed in the hands of a single officer who controls all the forces available to oppose the landing. Most defenders have accepted this concept, at least in theory, but have been unable to achieve it in practice. The few exceptions include the defenses of Wake and Midway Islands early in World War II. The overall record not only supports a defensive organization based on the principle of unity of command but also suggests that the individual in command be a naval officer. Mirroring the command structure of the forces conducting the landing, command of the defense should shift to an army officer only when the enemy's landing force has established itself ashore to the degree that the operation has clearly changed from an amphibious operation to a land battle. Commanders planning a landing have no influence over how a defending enemy force chooses to structure its command relationships. By the wrong choice of their own command relationships, however, amphibious planners could inadvertently give up one of their greatest operational advantages: unity of command under naval leadership.

Sea Control and Air Superiority

For the most part, those who have had to defend against major landings have enjoyed neither sea control nor air superiority in the vicinity of the landing. This reality, which has been a major factor in the failure of most anti-landing defenses, has two related causes. First, virtually all practitioners of amphibious warfare have considered sea control and air superiority to be prerequisites to landing. Second, the amphibious attacker has the initiative. If control of the sea and air is not gained at least in the immediate area of a landing, the attacker can postpone or cancel the landing. The defender has no such option. The corollary, of course, is that a defender can usually deter a landing by maintaining air and sea control.

One trap into which amphibious commanders can easily fall involves their interpreting sea control and air superiority to mean absolute sea control and undisputed supremacy in the air. Ideally, an attacker would like to eliminate the enemy from the air over the projected beachhead before commencing the landing. Tarawa, Normandy, and Inchon are good examples where air supremacy was gained by the attackers under widely different conditions. Such absolute control is not always possible, however, and perhaps not even necessary. The landings at Salerno, Leyte Gulf, Okinawa, and the Falklands all succeeded in spite of determined opposition from the defenders' air forces. To insist on completely eliminating any air opposition before landing could unnecessarily deter some future landing.

A similar situation exists with respect to sea control during an amphibious assault. By the time of the Normandy invasion, the Allies had largely destroyed the German navy. The Germans were reduced to responding with mines, submarines, and small attack craft. Had the invasion of Japan taken place, the Japanese navy would have had no large surface ships to use in opposing the landings. Earlier, however, it had actively opposed or threatened most of the Allied landings in the SWPA and some in the central Pacific. The landings at Guadalcanal, Leyte, and Saipan were all carried out under naval threats that resulted in the sea battles of Savo Island, Leyte Gulf, and Philippine Sea, respectively.

Doctrine

Doctrine is another issue that has distinguished amphibious attackers from defenders. The British and Americans, who have conducted most of the large-scale landings in this century, have had formal doctrine for amphibious operations since the period between the two world wars. Most of those who have defended against landings have had no formal doctrine to guide them. The Japanese were one exception. They recognized the need for anti-landing doctrine relatively late in World War II and then spent the rest of the conflict trying to develop a doctrine that worked. The result was a series of documents laying out a doctrine that evolved from a defense at the water's edge to a defense in depth and, by the end of the war, back to a defense at the water's edge.

The reason for the disparity between attackers and defenders with respect to the perceived need for formal doctrine is not clear. It may relate to two factors, both of which reflect the naval character of amphibious operations. First, naval officers have generally recognized both the special problems associated with conducting landings and the status of amphibious operations as a distinct form of naval warfare. Most defenders, army officers, for the most part, seem to have regarded their defensive efforts as simply ground operations and applied standard land warfare defensive doctrine.

Second, most attackers have considered landings to be operations of choice that can be used to advantage when the proper circumstances arise. Anticipating such circumstances in advance, they thought through the problems associated with amphibious warfare and created appropriate doctrines. Defenders, on the other hand, have generally found themselves in positions that were never anticipated. Had war plans of the Germans, Japanese, North Koreans, and Argentines succeeded, as they obviously anticipated, they never would have needed defenses against enemy landings. The lesson for defenders in the future is that anti-landing doctrine is essential. Developing such doctrine requires a potential defender to consider the many problems of the defense ahead of time, instead of waiting to confront them at some beachhead. Amphibious planners today should be aware that future opponents might not be as remiss in this respect as have many past defenders.

Opposing Force Ratios

In dismissing the importance of Allied landings during World War II, Soviet Admiral Gorshkov noted that the success of those operations could be reduced to a matter of arithmetic. He thought that amphibious attackers simply overwhelmed the defenders. Refuting this assertion involves an analysis of at least three complex factors: (1) numbers of troops and units on each side, (2) the weapons available to the opposing forces, and (3) the relative quality of their troops and leaders. Details of such an analysis would require a book of its own, but a few basic observations can be made.

Conventional wisdom holds that an amphibious attacker, like its land counterpart, requires a strength advantage of about three to one over the defender at the point of attack. The overall attacking force does not necessarily have to be three times larger than the overall defending force. Part of the art of the attacker is skill in concentrating the needed force at the point of attack. In spite of this, modern amphibious assaults have succeeded with a wide range of force ratios at the point of attack. At Tarawa, one of the most fiercely opposed landings in history, the 2d Marine Division succeeded with a numerical advantage of about two to one over the Japanese. At Sicily, a landing that one Soviet author called "an operation without risk," the Allies assaulted with nine divisions against a defending force of eleven.

The landing on Sicily, however, points out the effect that varying qualities of troops can have on a battle. General Guzzoni, the Axis commander, estimated before the battle that an American division represented the combat power of two German divisions or four Italian divisions. The outcome of the landing seems to have proved General Guzzoni right. Field Marshal Kesselring, overall German commander in Italy, said later that the armored attacks against the American beachhead at Gela would have succeeded had it not been for the determined resistance of a small number of American paratroopers from the 82d Airborne Division. Similarly, it is difficult to imagine that less skilled and determined troops than those of the U.S. Marine Corps would have been able to prevail at such heavily opposed landings as those on Tarawa, Peleliu, and Iwo Jima. At the same time, the history of modern amphibious warfare provides examples of forces of all calibers, elite to undistinguished, landing successfully against defenders of greatly varying quality.

During World War II, the attackers had the advantage of learning from firsthand experience. Three American divisions—1st and 4th Marine Divisions and 3d Infantry Division—each took part in four major landings. A number of others participated in more than one. Obviously, not every member of those divisions made every landing, but the collective experience of each division improved from operation to operation. The defenders, on the other hand, experienced quite different circumstances. With the major exception of some German divisions during the Italian campaign, each division of the defenders generally opposed only one landing.

The implications of opposing force ratios are particularly important to the future of U.S. amphibious operations. Since the Vietnam War, the requirement to apply overwhelming force has become an article of faith for American military planners. Although not precisely defined, overwhelming force would imply something greater than the three-to-one superiority normally accepted as necessary for a successful attack. This perceived need for overwhelming force, combined with the limited number of amphibious ships in the U.S. Navy, has the potential to deter operational commanders from making future landings against all but the weakest of opposing forces.

Risk and Casualties

Amphibious operations have the reputation of being particularly risky and costly in terms of casualties. Unfortunately, the reputation is based largely on a few landings that match this popular perception. Certain landings have produced exceptionally high casualty rates for the attackers; Dieppe, Tarawa, and Omaha Beach at Normandy come to mind. At Guadalcanal and Okinawa, landing forces came ashore unscathed because the enemy chose not to contest the landings. In the land battles that followed these two landings, the attackers suffered casualties, with particularly large numbers at Okinawa. The high casualty rates resulted from a variety of factors, however; only a few were related specifically to the nature of amphibious warfare.

The American public has always been sensitive to casualties in war. Realizing this, the Japanese attempted to exploit this sensitivity in their plans to defend against U.S. landings. The Japanese continued to hope that if they could inflict high enough casualties on American landing forces, the United States would reconsider its policy of unconditional surrender. That strategy failed during World War II, but it might well succeed today. An enemy of the United States, if anticipating a possible amphibious operation against its shores, might be able to deter it by creating the specter of massive American casualties.

The solution to this potential problem is psychological, not technical or tactical. U.S. military leaders must be able to calculate realistically the risks of military operations and then be willing to press civilian decision makers to authorize those operations in which the potential benefits outweigh the risks, including the risk of casualties. MacArthur did exactly that at Inchon. Although one pessimistic general rated the operation as a "5,000-to-1 shot," MacArthur informed the disturbed joint chiefs of staff that he regarded the chance of success to be "excellent." The mood of the American public today and the precedent of the Gulf War of 1991, with its extremely low casualty rate, have made the U.S. military averse to all but the slightest risk. Unfortunately, these two factors also give an enemy a perfect strategy for deterring or defending against an American amphibious operation.

The Impact of Delay

In the past, delay on the part of an attacker in carrying out a landing has almost always worked to the advantage of the defender. The reason for this is not entirely clear, but part of the explanation might be that the timing of a landing is frequently dictated by periodic conditions involving tide, daylight, and weather. An attacker who misses one opportunity could be forced to wait a month or more for the appropriate conditions to recur. If the attacking force has reached a peak of physical and psychological readiness, any delay could cause its readiness to diminish, rather than increase. A defender, on the other hand, would regard any delay as a temporary reprieve and take advantage of it to lay more mines, build more obstacles and fortifications, and generally improve the defense. Although the timing of a landing is largely in the hands of the attacker, an astute defender might find ways of frightening an opponent suspected of preparing a landing into delaying its execution.

The Impact of Improved Weapons

In the past, the advent of important new weapons, such as the machine gun, the quick-firing cannon, the airplane, and precision-guided weapons usually has been accompanied by predictions of the resulting demise of amphibious warfare. Invariably, these predictions have been proved wrong. There is no apparent reason to believe that similar predictions in the future will be any more accurate with respect to conventional weapons. The issue remains unresolved, however, regarding two special types of weapons: chemical and nuclear.

Chemical weapons have been a factor in warfare since World War I. Although banned by several international conventions, chemical weapons remain a potential threat to amphibious operations. Despite this, no defenders have attempted to defeat a landing by resorting to chemical warfare. Their reasons probably involve factors that are not strictly related to amphibious warfare, including the fear of retaliation and the reluctance of most nations to violate international laws of war. The question of chemical warfare arose during the Gulf War because Iraq was known to have chemical warfare capability. Iraq did not overtly employ chemical warfare forces during the war and might not have used gas against a landing had the United States conducted one.

In spite of the record, prudence requires that amphibious planners take chemical warfare into consideration. Protective measures for a landing force are necessary, but they deal with only half the problem. An amphibious attacker who lacks the capability of responding in kind to the use of chemical weapons by an enemy gives that enemy a powerful advantage. By selective use of chemical weapons, the defender could force the attacking forces to land in full protective suits, while the defender's troops remain free of such encumbrances. Because the United States is in the process of dismantling its retaliatory chemical warfare capability, the use or threat of chemical warfare will become more attractive to future defenders. The implication for amphibious planners is twofold.

First, U.S. amphibious forces must be capable of operating in a chemical environment. Second, lacking a retaliatory chemical capability, the United States must decide how to deter a future enemy's use of chemical warfare and how to respond if deterrence fails.

A similar set of uncertainties applies to the use of nuclear weapons to defeat a landing. In a narrow sense, nuclear weapons could have solved a variety of tactical problems since the end of World War II, but the cost of unleashing nuclear warfare far outweighs any potential benefits from doing so. The United States briefly considered their use during the Korean War and again at Dien Bien Phu to prevent a French defeat in Indochina. The reason why these weapons have not been used since World War II involve high-level strategic, political, legal, and moral considerations, not tactical or operational ones. So far, these high-level considerations have deterred the use of nuclear weapons by the few nations that possess them. Whether such restraint will continue as smaller, perhaps less responsible, nations develop nuclear capability is an open question.

Rather than allow a nuclear threat to deter future amphibious operations, the United States can pursue two courses of actions. The first course is to continue the development of dispersed amphibious operations that began with the use of helicopters after World War II. Such techniques offer the potential for a landing to succeed in spite of the use of a small number of low-yield tactical nuclear weapons by a defender. The second course is a statement by the United States that clearly delineates a policy regarding nuclear retaliation if nuclear weapons are ever used against American forces.

Mine Warfare

In a practical sense, naval mines constitute a much greater threat to amphibious operations today than either chemical or nuclear weapons. By modern standards, even the most sophisticated mines are relatively simple devices. They can be stockpiled during peacetime and laid with relative ease when needed. In spite of their relative simplicity, mines cause disproportionate problems for an attacker. Clearing a minefield for a landing is a slow process at best. An enemy could use the time gained to reposition forces and improve defenses. The damage to two U.S. warships off Kuwait by Iraqi contact mines during the Gulf War demonstrated the power of even a small-scale mine defense. Any nation threatened by amphibious attack today should clearly place naval mines high on its list of defensive priorities.

The lessons for the U.S. Navy are equally clear. Mine countermeasures must be considered an integral part of any amphibious operation. Unless the navy develops and maintains the ability to locate and sweep mines rapidly and on a relatively large scale, potential enemies will be able to deter the world's most powerful amphibious force. Some military planners might argue that the use of helicopters and air cushion landing craft (LCAC) has largely obviated the threat of mines to a landing. Although these two developments have reduced the threat, they have not eliminated it. For some time, the limited number of available LCACs will require amphibious forces to rely on conventional landing craft to deliver heavy equipment, such as tanks and self-propelled artillery, to a landing beach. Unless they are cleared, mines also can restrict the ability of amphibious ships to position themselves to launch amphibious vehicles or helicopters and can reduce the effectiveness of naval gunfire support by keeping ships far offshore.

Naval Gunfire

In the view of defenders against landings, naval gunfire, of all the weapons and techniques employed by amphibious attackers in modem landings, stands in a class of its own. The tremendous power of naval gunfire has been a common thread running through the accounts of defenders, including those from Turkey, Germany, Japan, and Argentina. Some military historians argue that this professed respect for naval gunfire is simply an excuse offered by defenders to deflect attention from their poor performance in other aspects of the defense. If so, it has been a recurrent, widely used excuse. Field Marshals Liman von Sanders, Kesselring, and Rommel and Generals Saito, Westphal, and von Senger und Etterlin, to name a few, highlight naval gunfire in their memoirs and after-action reports as an important factor in their defeats.

In the past, naval gunfire has played a role in neutralizing defensive troops on beaches; smashing coastal defense batteries, pillboxes, and other emplacements; and breaking up counterattacks, including those by armored forces. Today, however, defenders are largely free from worry about dealing with an attacker's naval gunfire. The largest gun currently in the U.S. Navy's arsenal is the 5-inch/54 caliber. Other navies are in no better shape. Gone are the 8-inch guns that were available through Vietnam and the 16-inch battleship guns that fired their last rounds during the Gulf War. Modem developments, such as base-bleed and rocketassisted shells to extend range, along with "smart" munitions to increase accuracy, ostensibly have allowed the 5-inch gun to carry out missions that previously required larger calibers. Unfortunately, that argument is only partially true. Regardless of its accuracy, a 5-inch shell can pack only a limited punch.

During World War II, the Germans and Japanese both constructed concrete coastal fortifications that could be destroyed only by repeated hits from naval guns of the heaviest caliber. Once again, the absence of such guns could make a defense at the water's edge a practical option for a defender willing to invest in coastal fortifications.

Missiles, such as the Tomahawk, could assume the point-destruction role of naval gunfire, but their use poses an economic question. In the past, American amphibious forces have landed against defenses that included hundreds of concrete emplacements. In the Pacific, naval guns systematically reduced these positions to rubble before a landing. Given the cost of modern missiles, the U.S. Navy is unlikely to maintain enough of them to use in the role previously performed by heavy naval gunfire.

World War II landings also demonstrated the need to neutralize enemy forces defending a beach before H-hour. To accomplish this mission, the British and Americans both developed vessels that could blanket a beach with tons of explosives delivered by rockets. The U.S. Navy lost this capability in the 1970s when it broke up or sold its few remaining rocket ships. This lost capability might be regained by mounting rocket launchers on amphibious ships. The

Soviet navy used this approach. In the U.S. Navy, this idea is still in the conceptual stage.

Along with marginal mine countermeasures, the lack of naval gunfire may be the greatest weakness of U.S. amphibious capabilities today. Some military theorists argue that the current lack of naval guns can be overcome by the increased use of air support, including support from air force bombers. The experience of World War II would indicate otherwise.

Target Priorities

One problem that has consistently confounded defenders who have attempted to use a naval defense against landings is the assignment of target priorities. In this respect, three classes of ships have generally vied for the highest priority: aircraft carriers, heavy naval gunfire ships, and transports and other amphibious ships that carry the landing force. More often than not, defenders have devoted their attention mainly to the first two categories. In some cases, this attention was an effort to reduce the impact of air strikes and naval gunfire on the defender. Two examples are Hitler's order for German forces to attack Allied battleships at Normandy and the Japanese navy's decision to use kamikazes against American carriers at Leyte Gulf. In other cases, defenders have chosen to attack the first available targets, which frequently were warships, not transports. This occurred regularly during the kamikaze attacks at Okinawa and Argentine air attacks against the British fleet during the Falklands operation. In still other cases, such target priorities have resulted from the belief—common in the Japanese navy during World War II—that warships are more worthy targets for attack than transports or other ships.

By the end of World War II, the Japanese had adopted a more pragmatic approach that could serve as the model for any anti-landing defense. In this model, the amphibious ships are by far the highest priority targets. When an amphibious ship, with its embarked landing force, is sunk, neither the ship nor the landing force can participate in a landing, irrespective of how much damage the supporting carriers and naval gunfire ships inflict on the defender. In Clausewitzian terms, the amphibious ships are the attacker's center of gravity.

Destroying that center is the defender's most certain way of defeating the landing. There are exceptions; in the Falklands, for example, the British carriers were as crucial to the landing as the amphibious ships. Realizing their importance, Admiral Woodward protected both carriers and troop transports, even when this increased the risk to other elements of the task force.

Summary

The record of amphibious warfare in the twentieth century seems to validate Sir Walter Raleigh's assessment that defending against an amphibious operation is more difficult than conducting one. In spite of the record, many military theorists continue to hold that an assault landing against a defended beach is no longer a feasible operation of war and that the United States should rely solely on a MacArthur-like approach of landing where the enemy "ain't." Such an approach would reduce the equipment needs of the U.S. Marine Corps and naval amphibious forces and largely obviate the necessity to replace large-caliber naval gunfire.

Landing at a location that is not a strongly defended one has always been the preferred option. During World War II, the Germans and Japanese were frequently unwilling to make such an option available. Those theorists who dispute the need to conduct opposed landings in the future are saying, in effect, that because they cannot envision any circumstances that would require another Tarawa or Normandy, no such circumstances will ever exist.

The severe limitations of an amphibious force with the inability to conduct an opposed landing offer a critical advantage to a defender. Against such a force, a defender can use a defense at the water's edge to protect selected landing beaches. Knowing that the attacker will not be able to land at the defended beaches, the defender's mobile forces are free to concentrate on those "undefended" areas where the enemy might be able to land. A force trained and equipped to land across a defended beach can always land across an undefended one, but the reverse is not true.

In the final analysis, the amphibious attack has been proved a stronger operation of war than the anti-landing defense. Some of the reasons for this superiority, such as the initiative that accrues to any attacker and the superior mobility of naval forces, can be attributed to the nature of the amphibious operation itself. Most of the reasons are not inherent, however, but result from a nation's willingness to maintain the tools of this specialized form of naval warfare and to accept the risks of using it when necessary.

Americans can always refuse to pay the price for maintaining an amphibious capability, thereby giving up what Liddell Hart calls "the greatest strategic asset that a sea-based power possesses." If Americans should choose to take such a step, they will have, in effect, accomplished what no enemy has managed to do: defeat a modern amphibious operation.

12 "EFFECT OF THE MARINES ON THE NAVY"

(Selection from chapter 9 of *Battle Line*)

Thomas C. Hone and Trent Hone

This chapter from *Battle Line* describes the effects the Marines had on the Navy while both prepared for World War II. It concisely relates the often-told story of the evolution of amphibious operations, from the British failure after getting ashore at Gallipoli in World War I to the many successful amphibious operations in World War II.

We got off to a slow start throughout the 1920s while Marine Corps thinking and Naval War College games against Japan together established the need for amphibious doctrine, experiments, and new technologies. Then in a rush during the 1930s, prewar plans came to fruition just in time to create the means for successful Marine assaults, small ones in the first landings at Guadalcanal and Tulagi, a fierce one at Tarawa, and large, fierce ones at Saipan, Peleliu, and Iwo Jima. Meanwhile, the lessons learned in the Atlantic theater and a growing set of amphibious forces facilitated large Army landings in North Africa and Europe, culminating in the unparalleled scope of the D-day assault in June 1944. Toward the end of the war in the Pacific, the defending Japanese had learned how better to resist large Army-Marine landings in the Philippines and Okinawa. Tom and Trent Hone describe what it took, in doctrine, leadership, ships, landing craft, aircraft, and other substance, to get the Navy-Marine Corps team ready for World War II, and with no time to spare.

The Hones' chapter on the Navy-Marine connection was a difficult choice for me because there are other rich chapters in *Battle Line* describing what it took to develop other tactics and technologies between the World Wars. Tom Hone is a respected expert on the peacetime advancement of naval aviation in the U.S. Navy, the Royal Navy, and the Imperial Japanese Navy. The chapter is superb in reporting the aggressive U.S. Navy support for carrier development before World War II, the relatively generous funding, the widespread uncertainties about aircraft roles and missions to include dirigibles and amphibians, and the just-in-time development of power plants sufficient to carry the bomb and torpedo payloads to a range that ensured carrier air dominance over battleships from the onset of the war.

A different chapter on submarine peacetime development is equally valuable. Submarine tactics against shipping were rudimentary at the outset of the war, so it took time for our boats to learn the art of deployment for a series of solo engagements that, cumulatively, were phenomenally successful in destroying Japanese shipping.

"EFFECT OF THE MARINES ON THE NAVY"
(Selection from chapter 9 of *Battle Line: The United States Navy 1919–1939*) by Thomas C. Hone and Trent Hone (Naval Institute Press, 2006): 145–56.

> Under no circumstances shall any Marine enlisted man be employed as a servant.—*U.S. Navy Regulations, 1920*

> "Good-by," I said. "Maybe you need a little help."
> I shook myself like a wet dog. "I need a company of marines . . ."
> —Raymond Chandler, *Farewell My Lovely*

The Marine Corps has a unique place in American history. It is a hallowed organization. Its saints are common soldiers, most not far beyond adolescence.

Some were just boys when they waged the terrible battles that took their lives or shook what humanity they had to its roots. Students of their struggles (some of the better of them Marines themselves) have produced fascinating, thoughtful histories of their campaigns, and the Corps itself (especially its many veterans) has kept charge of an extraordinarily potent myth.

By comparison, this chapter will take its lead from a point Vice Admiral George C. Dyer made in 1966: "Since most of the books devoting any large amount of space to . . . amphibious doctrine have been sponsored by the Marine Corps or written by Marines, it is perhaps natural that the work and contributions . . . of various other parts of the Department of the Navy . . . have not been stressed." In this chapter we will attempt to cover those contributions. We will also suggest, however, that the implications of the amphibious doctrine developed by the Marine Corps in the 1930s did not gain the attention within the Navy that they deserved. That was partly because of timing; amphibious doctrine came along rather late in the interwar period. But it was also because the Navy just did not realize how important an effective, *standing* amphibious force was to war at sea. The Marine Corps remade itself in the years between World War I and World War II. For example, *U.S. Navy Regulations, 1920* defined the duties of the Marine Corps as follows:

(a) To furnish organizations for duty afloat . . .

(b) To garrison the different navy yards and naval stations . . .

(c) To furnish the first line of the mobile defenses of naval bases and stations beyond the continental limits of the United States.

(d) To man such naval defenses . . . as may be erected for the defense of naval bases and naval stations beyond the continental limits of the United States.

(e) To furnish such garrisons and expeditionary forces for duties beyond the seas as may be necessary in time of peace.

Yet in 1921, Major Earl H. Ellis convinced the commandant of the Marine Corps to accept a different statement of the mission of the Corps:

In order to impose our will upon Japan, it will be necessary for us to project our fleet and land forces across the Pacific and wage war in Japanese waters. To effect this requires that we have sufficient bases to support the fleet, both during its projecting and afterwards. As the matter stands at present, we cannot count upon the use of any bases west of Hawaii except those which we may seize from the enemy after the opening of hostilities.

The history of the Marine Corps in the 1920s and 1930s is therefore a history of an organization changing itself. And, as the Marines changed, the Navy had to follow. The Marines became an amphibious force *within* the Navy, and, in so doing, began a process of changing the Navy, too. The dramatic implications of this change from within weren't obvious at the time. It took a war to get naval officers to realize that large-scale, successful amphibious warfare gave the Navy and the nation a new and powerful strategic tool.

In 1921, Marines (and sailors, too) were prepared to foray ashore for raids, or to rescue endangered American citizens, or to establish a base for the Navy in wartime (as Marines had done at Guantanamo Bay in the Spanish-American War). But Ellis grasped that what came to be called "amphibious warfare" was much more than the occasional raid. It was the use of forces from the sea to achieve decisive results in major land campaigns. The British had tried just such a move at Gallipoli in 1915—and had failed. Ellis and his colleagues in the Marine Corps had to demonstrate that a major amphibious campaign could succeed.

British forces had a long history of using the sea as a means of moving troops to attack or harass a land-based enemy army at a weak point. In the eighteenth and nineteenth centuries, navies had much greater strategic mobility than armies, and Britain's Royal Navy could use that mobility to gain a tactical advantage for England's small army that offset its relatively modest size. Someone once said that the Royal Navy could therefore be likened to a cannon that fired a "shell" called the British army. The failed amphibious campaign against Turkish forces at Gallipoli in World War I discredited this simile. The Marines set out, in the 1920s and 1930s, to restore it—for the United States.

Others have told the story of how this was done in detail. The studies of Gallipoli and related campaigns led to a series of exercises with the fleet and even with the Army in the 1920s. Marines conducted a mock amphibious assault on the Panama Canal in 1923, and tests of amphibious equipment and tactics on Culebra Island, Puerto Rico, the following year. A major Army, Navy, and Marine Corps exercise was staged on Oahu, Hawaii, in 1925. The goal was to determine whether the assaults that were part of the "Orange" trans-Pacific war plan were feasible.

The assessment of the results of these exercises led directly to a new statement of tactical Marine Corps doctrine: the *Tentative Manual for Landing Operations* of 1934. The *Tentative Manual* overcame the division between sea and shore that had so bedeviled the British at Gallipoli by abolishing it:

> A landing operation against opposition is, in effect, an assault on an organized or unorganized defensive position modified by substituting initially ships' gunfire for that of light, medium, and heavy field artillery, and frequently, carrier-based aviation for land-based air units until the latter can be operated from shore.

This doctrine was revolutionary. It did not just say that the Navy would move the Marines (or the Army) from place to place in order to surprise an enemy. It also did not say that fleet gunfire and air operations would be used temporarily to back up a raid. Instead, it said that the reason why the British failed was because they did not treat the fleet as a source of organic support for the land forces. Put another way, the Marine Corps developed a doctrine that required the Marine Corps "tail" to wag the Navy "dog" instead of the other way around.

According to Vice Admiral Dyer, none of this would have happened without the support of senior Navy officers, especially Admiral Robert E. Coontz, Chief of Naval Operations and then Commander-in-Chief of the U.S. Fleet. In 1925, for example, Coontz recognized that landing operations placed a special burden on the Navy—that of designing special landing craft, providing gunfire support on a continuing basis for Marines assaulting a hostile shore, and systematically training officers to handle the boats carrying Marine infantry to a defended beach.

This new set of *naval* requirements generated conflict between the Navy and the Marines on two levels. The first was over the details of the Orange plan for war against Japan. As Edward S. Miller revealed in his detailed study of pre-World War II Pacific war planning, the Marines immediately took Navy plans for attacks on Japanese-held islands and began drawing from them their force and tactical requirements. How many Marines would be needed for the assaults? What support would they require from the Navy? Who would defend an island after the Marines captured it? Marine planners worked backward from the operational goals set by their Navy counterparts in the Office of the Chief of Naval Operations.

The numbers they came up with stunned Navy commanders. In 1935, for example, Marine planners considering assaults on the Marshall Islands wanted half the Navy's battleships for artillery support and all the active carriers to gain air superiority over the Marshalls themselves. But how could the Navy assign such forces to an amphibious campaign when they knew the Imperial Fleet would be thundering down on what was left of the U.S. Fleet, eager for *the* decisive battle at sea? In front of the General Board in 1938, Marine officers argued for more land-based aircraft for their assault forces, even if getting those aircraft meant taking them from what the naval aviators thought was their minimum requirement. Marines also asked for dedicated ships to move their own aviation units forward with their assault forces. The Navy balked at such requests, even when Army war planners offered new long-range aircraft such as the B-17 to shield amphibious operations from attack by Japanese naval forces.

As Miller found, "The navy remained adamant that the carriers must roam free." But as Miller also discovered, trying to resolve the seeming impasse that divided Navy and Marine Corps planners led to some breakthroughs. First, planners abandoned the idea that they should capture most islands in a cluster. If it were necessary to take and hold a base in the Marshalls, then one or two islands would do. American aviation could keep the Japanese from reinforcing the rest. Second, the island stepping-stones to Japanese home waters would have to be selected from among those that land-based aviation could reach. Instead of using bombers such as the B-17 to shield amphibious assaults, the Navy's carriers would shield the bomber bases with its carriers, and the bombers would pummel Japanese island bases and defenses.

The second level of conflict between the Marines and the Navy focused on particulars. In landing exercises on Oahu in 1932, the participants discovered a number of obstacles to conducting a successful amphibious assault. Ships' boats, for example, were inadequate landing craft for heavily armed Marines who expected to land in the face of enemy defenses. Even the fifty-foot motor launches carried by battleships had problems putting Marines ashore in any kind of surf and pulling off again.

This prompted both the Navy and the Marines to search for new forms of landing craft. The Navy pursued and tested its own designs as well as commercial offerings that might be adapted to mass production. Exercises with prototypes showed that the problem of developing suitable landing craft was not a minor one. As historian Leo J. Daugherty III found, the Marines realized that they needed landing craft for personnel, "lighters" for vehicles and tanks, and amphibious vehicles that could "swim" ashore on their own. The Marines also needed specially designed amphibious transports. The Navy only had one—*Henderson*, built during World War I—and that was clearly not enough.

To make sure that the Marines got their landing craft, Secretary of the Navy Claude Swanson established the senior Continuing Board for the Development of Landing Boats for Training in Landing Operations in January 1937. Admiral Arthur J. Hepburn, the Fleet Commander, set up the Fleet Development Board to oversee the testing of the landing craft that were bought commercially or produced to a Navy design. For the next three years, Navy and Marine Corps officers tried to find landing craft that met their requirements. Seeing Japanese forces use such craft effectively near Shanghai in 1937 provoked the Marine Corps to put extra pressure on the Navy, but the process of finding suitable landing craft was not successful until 1940, when the Navy procured numbers of the soon-to-be-famous Higgins Boats.

In later years, Andrew J. Higgins, who had created the firm that produced the best landing craft of the crop of commercial boats that the Navy tested, claimed that first the Bureau of Construction and Repair and then its successor, the Bureau of Ships, had deliberately tried to avoid buying his shallow-water craft. That may be; the evidence is mixed. But two points should be kept in mind. First, the Navy paid for and staged a series of increasingly sophisticated fleet landing exercises from 1935 through 1941. These exercises tested equipment (including landing craft and radios), doctrine (for fire support from planes and ships), and tactics (whether night landings were safer than those in daylight, for example).

Second, Navy officers did not lose sight of the need to support the Marines. The decisions of Admiral Coontz have already been mentioned. Another, later, case was when Admiral Edward C. Kalbfus brought the "Alligator" amphibious tractor to the attention of his Marine colleagues. The tractor, based on a commercially produced vehicle designed to navigate the Florida Everglades, was the third piece of the puzzle of getting the Marines ashore. Supporting them once they got there also posed problems for the Navy. At first glance, battleships seemed ideal gunfire support ships. Their 14- and 16-inch guns appeared powerful enough to smash almost any land defenses. However, for Navy battleships to provide amphibious operations with effective gunfire support, they had to have shells that were *not* armor piercing.

The armor-piercing shells, designed to break through dense armor plate, were mostly metal. For example, the 14-inch, 50-caliber armor-piercing shell fired by *Tennessee* in the 1920s had an explosive filler that weighed only 29.5 pounds. The shell weighed a total of 1,400 pounds. The filler was only 2.1 percent of the projectile's weight. The heavier 1,500-pound shell developed by the Bureau of Ordnance in the 1930s had an explosive charge that weighed only 22.5 pounds, or 1.5 percent of the projectile's total weight.

The heavy, dense shells were designed to crash through an enemy's thick armor plates and *then* explode. Explosive force was traded off to increase the chance that the shell would break through armor. The "high capacity" or "bombardment" shells, by contrast, were of lighter construction overall, were fused to burst on impact, and carried a heavier bursting charge. The Mk. 9 for the 14-inch, 50-caliber gun weighed 1,410 pounds and carried an explosive filler weighing 105 pounds. About 7.5 percent of the shell's total weight, and much more of its internal volume, was devoted to its explosive charge.

Assuming that the bombardment shells worked as intended, battleships could strike effectively at those targets ashore that their guns could reach. Ship-to-shore gunfire was tested in all the fleet landing exercises from 1935 until the last of the prewar maneuvers in the spring of 1941. The lessons learned were significant. The need for special bombardment ammunition became very clear very quickly. So, too, were the effects of the various shells: from the larger, heavier ones down to the 5-inch and 4-inch ones fired by destroyers. Gunfire was controlled effectively from the air and from fire control parties ashore. In addition, as one report noted, "fire can be rapidly and effectively shifted at any time, to any target, subject to the limitation [i.e., range] of the particular projectile."

Most important, however, was the lesson learned about coordination: the actions of planes, ships firing at land targets, transports, and assault boats could be conducted successfully "on a strict time schedule." That meant the challenge of Gallipoli had been overcome—Marines could assault a *defended* beach. Unfortunately, there was no funding to conduct full-scale tests. Ships didn't fire what the Army considered an adequate barrage (equal to sixteen 75-mm shells per minute in a one hundred yard square for three consecutive minutes) until 1938. Moreover, the ships—especially the battleships—engaged in fire support exercises tended *not* to be first line units. Even in 1939, the battleships firing at shore targets were *Texas, New York*, and *Wyoming*, and the last of these had been partially disarmed in accordance with the provisions of the London Naval Treaty of 1930.

There was another issue that the landing exercises didn't resolve: What should be the mix of armor-piercing and bombardment shells in a battleship's magazines? *Tennessee* carried a maximum of twelve hundred 14-inch shells, or one hundred for each of her twelve big guns. That may sound like a lot, but it is not—not in a heavy engagement, whether against enemy defenses on land or against enemy ships at sea. In peacetime, however, there was not enough money to pay for a battleship to empty her magazines by continuous firing, so no one knew just what the rate of sustained fire would be in a fleet engagement, and therefore there was no telling just what the mix of shells (armor-piercing and bombardment) should be in a battleship's magazine. It also wasn't clear how much replenishment the battleships would need if they spent several days pounding a defended beach before a Marine assault.

In World War II, when money was no longer a problem, Fleet Commander Admiral Ernest J. King ordered *Idaho* (BB-42) to find out. As Norman Friedman learned, *Idaho* "actually fired off 100 rounds per gun of her two forward turrets on the morning of 10 October 1942." Of the 156 salvos fired, in only twenty were all six guns in the two forward turrets fired together. As Friedman learned, "more often (forty-seven times) five of the six could fire together. . . . On average the interval between salvoes was 1 minute 24 seconds. However, a 5-gun salvo was fired only forty-nine seconds after the previous salvo, and salvoes sixty to eighty, mostly 5-gun salvoes, were fired at an average interval of sixty-seven seconds." That is, it took just over a minute to level the guns, open the breeches, ram home shell and powder bags separately, close the breeches, elevate the guns, and get off the next salvo.

This exercise proved that battleships could indeed sustain high rates of fire, and it would not take long for them to empty their magazines. How, then, should they be loaded for an amphibious operation? If Japanese battleships came out to fight and ships such as *Idaho* carried mostly non-armor-piercing shells, the whole operation—never mind how the Marines were doing ashore—would be in grave danger. But if the battleships did not carry enough bombardment shells, then the Marine assault might be defeated. Or, if it succeeded, the cost in casualties might be so terrible that there would not be enough Marines left for further attacks. Remember that there were only 14,500 Marines in 1934 and just over 17,000 five years later. Individual Marines were (and remained) a scarce resource until war began.

The distribution of shells between armor-piercing and bombardment would not matter as much if fresh supplies were always at hand, but nothing like that could be guaranteed the fleet in the 1930s, and that is one reason the chiefs of Naval Operations in that decade wanted many more auxiliaries (tankers, tenders, supply ships, and so forth) in the fleet. It is also why gunfire exercises in support of operations ashore did not reveal all the problems that would arise in World War II. There just wasn't money to pay for such an expenditure of shells.

By 1939, however, progress was being made in all the areas identified by the Marines in 1935 except one—the development of a unique amphibious command ship. The reason for this lapse (which would be corrected in World War II) was that the naval part of an amphibious operation was placed under the command of a naval officer. It was assumed that the Marine Corps commander would assume command of his ground and air forces after the former had secured enough of a foothold ashore to support his command staff and their equipment. Not well understood was the need to have a joint command that would stay together for the duration of the amphibious operation on a ship dedicated to that mission. The danger—and the Marines were aware of it in the 1930s—was that the Navy ships and aircraft supporting them would pull out and head for the enemy if scouts detected the approach of the Imperial Japanese Navy.

This fear of being left without support was one reason why Marine Corps leaders pressed so emphatically and persistently for their own air force. In the fall of 1932, for example, Marine aviation consisted of eight squadrons (eighty-eight aircraft). Most (forty-eight) were observation planes, assigned the task of spotting gunfire and finding the enemy. Only twenty-two were fighters. The rest were utility aircraft and transports. But all were active. Elements of the two fighting squadrons and twelve observation aircraft had flown off carriers *Lexington* (CV-2) and *Saratoga* (CV-3) in the summer of 1931. Many of the remaining observation planes and most of the eight transports had deployed to Nicaragua or Haiti to support Marine ground units. By the summer of 1938, there were 143 active aircraft in eleven squadrons, but, as in 1932, only two of the eleven squadrons were composed of fighters. Moreover, the only regular overseas deployment was to St. Thomas in the Virgin Islands.

One problem facing Marine Corps aviation was how to get to the fight. As early as 1928, the Marines had asked for a small carrier or at least a specialized aircraft transport. Their leaders were quite aware that the Navy was, because of treaty restrictions, short of aircraft carriers, but the Marines did not want to stage an assault without their own aircraft in support. For its part, the Navy did not want to see any of its scarce and essential carrier tonnage corralled by the Marines. This conflict continued into the early part of 1940, with the Chief of the Bureau of Aeronautics, Rear Admiral John H. Towers, rejecting a proposal for a special seagoing tender for Marine Corps combat aircraft.

However, the exposure of Marine pilots and their ground crews to Navy procedures had some positive effects. In 1968, retired Marine Brigadier General Edward C. Dyer, who served with one of the Marine detachments sent to a carrier, recalled that his experience was

> a rude awakening. . . . There was no monkey business whatsoever. In the first place we were handed a doctrine, a book, a guide, that told us how the squadron should be organized. . . . The organization and operation of the squadron was definitely controlled. . . . All of our material was requisitioned and accounted for. We were required to follow a training syllabus. We had so many hours of gunnery, so many hours of navigation, so many hours of radio practice, so many hours of formation flying, so many hours of night flying, and we jolly well had to do it.

They were part of the Navy, and the Navy was a "fighting machine."

The development of the Fleet Marine Force was an innovation equal to that of naval aviation in importance. Though that force started small—one regiment of infantry and supporting artillery—it advanced in both size and sophistication in much the same way as naval aviation advanced. Marine Corps officers studied the problems of amphibious operations, then drafted tentative doctrine covering such operations, and finally tested that doctrine in a series of exercises. Lessons learned in the exercises were plowed back into the doctrine and also used as the basis for decisions about the development of small landing craft and the purchase (after 1938) of amphibious tractors. This was basically the same cycle of thought, tests, and more thought that had proved so useful in naval aviation. Progress for the Marines, unfortunately, was constrained by a lack of funds to a degree that had not hampered naval aviation.

For example, in the same hearing before the General Board in 1938 when the Marine Corps representatives had asked for more aircraft, they noted that the difference between success and failure in storming a defended beach was the length of time that shells or bombs would *not* strike the defenders as the Marine landing craft approached. Clearly, the Navy's barrage had to stay ahead of the Marines if its shells were not to strike the Marines themselves. But the Marines wanted as much *close, organic* support as possible, and they thought they could get it only from their own air units; they therefore wanted a dedicated carrier. That's what they had learned from the limited number of exercises that a scarcity of funds had allowed, and that was just one piece of the larger tapestry of amphibious operations that they were weaving with the Navy.

The Navy, sadly, was slow to see this tapestry. The first concern of naval officers was to restore and modernize the fleet, especially the combat ships. The General Board, charged with advising the Secretary of the Navy on ship designs, reviewed most of the designs in the 1930s that would play such a major role in World War II—even including smaller ships such as minesweepers and net layers. Little attention, however, was devoted to amphibious transports, and none was given to the military potential of a permanent amphibious command ship.

As late as the spring of 1940, the board was reviewing two small but fast (sixteen knot) transports (APA-1 and APA-11) being designed specifically by the Maritime Commission for the Marines. The Marines had a set of requirements based on the lessons learned from the fleet landing exercises. They knew how much space they needed on these ships for gasoline, ammunition, vehicles, and combat troops. They knew how large the cargo hatches on the ships needed to be and how much deck space they needed on each ship so that they could assemble their men before transferring them to their landing craft. The Marines were happy to see the Maritime Commission designing the first purpose-built amphibious transports in a generation.

But the Navy bureau representatives admitted to the members of the General Board that they had not yet figured out how to get Marines off the decks of these transports and into their landing craft quickly and safely. They accepted the Marine Corps doctrine that Marine units had to be transferred from specialized transports to landing craft while beyond the range of short-range enemy defenses, but no one knew how to do this quickly while preserving the organization of the Marine assault units.

Navy officers testifying before the General Board also complained that smaller transports were less cost-efficient than larger ones, and they admitted that they had voluntarily passed the responsibility for carefully designing such ships to the Maritime Commission. Missing from the discussion was the careful attention to detail that the bureaus usually gave to issues of ship design. Also missing was an appreciation of the scale of construction that would be required in the event of a war in the Pacific. The OPNAV war planners were more or less on target with their estimates of the resources required for a Pacific amphibious campaign. The bureaus weren't nearly ready to support them in 1940, despite the reports of a series of useful fleet landing exercises.

Nonetheless, amphibious warfare changed the Navy profoundly. In 1939, for example, the Navy had only one amphibious transport designed as such—*Henderson*. By the end of 1944, the Navy had over eighty—and that doesn't count the *attack* transports (APAs, of which there were nearly two hundred) or the plethora of other, related ships that formed the Navy's huge amphibious force. Most of these ships were conversions of Maritime Commission designs, which demonstrates the importance of the Maritime Commission to the Navy. But the Navy also paid for the construction of thousands of large (the LST, or landing ship tank) and small (the thirty-six-foot Higgins Boat was just one of many) landing craft during the war—an armada that was, in effect, a navy of its own.

The Marines had chosen to affirm the commitment to the Navy that their most famous prewar commandant, Major General John A. Lejeune, had expressed in an essay in the *Naval Institute Proceedings* in October 1925. In that paper, Lejeune had argued that the Marine Corps "must ever be associated with the Navy, understanding the life at sea, the requirements and methods of naval warfare, and [be] imbued with the *esprit* of the naval service." Despite very real disputes between Navy and Marine Corps officers over funding and just how the fleet would sustain the Marines during amphibious operations, the prewar Marines did not entertain the idea that they would ever abandon their naval roots. To do so would have meant amalgamation with the Army, and that was an option Marine Corps officers chose not to consider, despite the problems being a part of the Navy caused them.

In the National Archives there is a photograph of a Marine enlisted radio operator on a bridge wing of battleship *Maryland* (BB-46) during the assault on Tarawa in November 1943. He was trying without success to sustain communication with assault troops pinned down by Japanese gunfire. *Maryland* did not have a communications division dedicated to and equipped properly for the assault, and individual Marines paid a terrible price for that lapse. Yet the need for such an organization with its own equipment had been made apparent by the prewar exercises. It is true, as Jeter Isely and Philip Crowl pointed out in their *The U.S. Marines and Amphibious War*, that "at the war's beginning, United States forces had at their disposal a body of tactical principles forming a basic amphibious doctrine which the test of warfare proved to be sound." But it's also true that the Marines, by accepting the limits of the Navy's budget and the process by which the Navy developed innovations, found themselves playing a deadly version of catch-up ball once war began.

13 "MISSILE CHESS: A PARABLE"

CAPT Wayne P. Hughes Jr., USN

I wrote this essay out of frustration over the lack of recognition that the missile era of warfare commenced on or about 1970 and the U.S. Navy was slow to understand the effect upon our queens of battle, our aircraft carriers, which have so much value the loss of even one would be a national tragedy.

If you believe chess has become too stereotyped from long study by people with unique intellects, then try missile chess for a new experience. It has different kinds of problems to solve and events to foresee, such as running out of missiles—a very real problem in the missile battles suffered by the Egyptians and Syrians in the 1973 Arab-Israeli War. Missile chess also has hints that some battles will be fought at closer range than is expected. It is said that when Admiral Arleigh Burke was given a tour of his new namesake, DDG-51, someone asked him if there was anything he would add to make it a complete fighting ship. Perhaps recalling his days leading DesRon 23 in battles of the upper Solomons at nearly point blank range, Burke said, "I think I would add a brace of cutlasses in the wardroom." To take a piece in missile chess you must occupy its square. This sounds, tongue in cheek, a lot like boarding the enemy with pistol and cutlass.

Missile chess is a useful parable of modern naval combat but a poor analogy. First, chess and missile chess are games of complete information. In real combat, success usually results from attacking at some risk, and certainly before you know as much as you see on a chess board about the enemy's formation and composition. Second, to match real missile warfare, the many low-value pawns should have the ability to attack a rook or a bishop when the enemy piece is still half of a chessboard away. Third and most important, a missile chess master under appropriate circumstances must have the power to attack with several pieces on the same move!

So don't take the parable as more than it is. It is a cautionary warning that missile warfare takes different forces and tactics to win because it is a different competition. As you read, be on the lookout for the White Queen suddenly racing out of the forest, pursued by we never learn what demons.

"Missile Chess" won honorable mention in the Naval Institute's General Prize essay competition of 1981.

"MISSILE CHESS: A PARABLE"

By CAPT Wayne P. Hughes Jr., USN, U.S. Naval Institute *Proceedings* (July 1981): 26–30.

> It's a great huge game of chess that's being played—all over the world—if this is the world at all. . . .—Lewis Carroll, *Through the Looking Glass*

Peacetime military planning is governed by analogy. The essence of readiness is combat training, which in peacetime is a sterile imitation of wartime experience. Strategy and tactics derive so much from extrapolations from the past that it is a popular half-truth that military men prepare for the last war. Weapons are designed in the mythological paper world of systems analysis and are tested in the tepid environment of safety-first.

In this peacetime world of pseudo-realism, fleet exercises and war games are the best simulations we have of the wartime world of blood, sweat, and courage. Yet fleet exercises are infrequent and expensive and have their own constraints: "Orange" commanders, for instance, will think like Americans, in spite of their best efforts to "think Red." War games are even greater abstractions, of which the most realistic and time-consuming will leave plenty of doubt over the influence of the "random number generator" and other artificialities.

Still, there are clues. After nearly all these exercises and games, the exercise reports say, in effect, "Missile magazine capacity might have been a problem." It is a vast understatement. The Israeli-Egyptian naval war of 1973 was characterized by deception, countermeasures, and tactics in which success or failure hinged on who had the last weapons remaining. The aircraft carrier has long been the backbone of U.S. Navy tactics for two reasons: aircraft radius of action and the capacity for sustained combat. An attack aircraft may rearm; a missile is on a one-way trip. To highlight their formidability, missiles have been likened to pilotless kamikazes. But the comparison also highlights their weakness: a missile can be used only once.

Let us imagine a test of the role that missile capacity will play in naval combat. We will keep the test absurdly simple and the analogy so remote that there can be no danger of inferring unwarranted conclusions. Let us devise a war game that is simple, replicative, and with characteristics that are generally understood by most military men.

Let us play chess.

We will make one change. We will give each piece two "shots." Each pawn and piece will have two chips, and when it takes another piece it spends one chip. After it has captured twice, it is out of weapons and becomes a passive participant—useful, you will learn when you play, to block and interpose but without the power to destroy. All the other rules of chess hold: castling, capturing *en passant*, checking and mating. A pawn reaching the eighth row is promoted and rearmed with two weapons.

Missile chess is different from regular chess. Just as the warrior who adapts to new weapons defeats the warrior who will not learn, so the missile chess player who understands the consequences of his new constraint will defeat the expert at classical chess. Pawns, armed like queens and rooks, become 8 feet tall, like a man on the frontier with a Colt .45. A knight, bishop, or any other piece may capture his way into a mating move and be powerless to execute the coup de grace. End games hinge on who has armed pawns and pieces remaining on the board.

There are untold variations. Missile Kriegspiel is one in which both sides maneuver without knowledge of the enemy's moves and a referee adjudicates, and if you believe that war is not war without the fog of uncertainty, then try it. But the most subtle change is to let both players distribute their 32 missiles among their pieces in any way they choose. Here we come to the nub of it. What is a winning distribution of offensive power? An effective approach is to arm the chessmen according to their mobility and maneuverability. Let us give the White king two missiles for self-defense, the majestic queen six, the formidable rooks four each, the bishops and knights two, and each of the pawns one. With this balance, White will usually defeat Black, whose missiles are uniformly allocated two per piece.[1] White must husband his queen and rooks until their greater capability can be brought to bear, so that as the game opens out toward the end, their sustained offensive power can be decisive. Black must rely heavily on his pawns, which are hampered by their lack of mobility. Black must be willing to sacrifice any piece or pawn to get at and trade off for White's queen and rooks. But as often as not, when Black achieves a breakthrough, he finds that his pieces are out of weapons and have become derelicts on the chessboard.

Does White resemble the U.S. Navy, with the great sustained offensive power of its aircraft carriers represented by the queen and rooks? Whatever one believes about the aptness of the comparison, it is evident that our Navy has not achieved the same balance that we have ascribed to the White chessmen. For the next several years at least, the U.S. Navy will have its offensive strength heavily concentrated in its carriers. It is a queenly strength unparalleled in range, sustained destructive power, and mobility. But we have 13 queens and 300 other pieces. Our 300 other warships are substantially less well armed for offense than White's bishops, knights, and pawns. To draw the analogy with the U.S. battle fleet more closely, one would have to:

- Superimpose the king on the queen, because the tactical commander rides the carrier.
- Remove the missiles from the bishops and knights, and devote them, like cruisers and guided missile destroyers, to the defense of the air-craft carriers—the rooks and queen.
- Remove half of the White pawns, to symbolize the diminishing number of surface combatants that we will have when they are armed with Harpoon, and, ultimately, Tomahawk.

One does not have to play missile chess to sense that the White chessmen so armed would lose. Their offensive power has been over-concentrated. When hapless White feels the frustration of having so much power bottled up in two rooks and a king-queen, harassed and nibbled at and finally destroyed by the relentless pursuit of Black's pawns and pieces, then he will see *Through the Looking Glass* what Alice saw:

"Look, look!" she cried, pointing eagerly.

"There's the White Queen running across the country! She came flying out of the woods over yonder—How fast those Queens can run!"

"There's some enemy after her, no doubt," the King said, without looking around. "The wood's full of them."

All of this presses the analogy too far, of course. Moreover, we have excluded all thought of amphibious warfare ships, minecraft, and many submarine and antisubmarine forces which would play out their roles on another gameboard. And yet . . . and yet . . . the essence of wisdom remains. One cannot play missile chess without the haunting premonition of an impending disaster for our Navy and our nation if we do not more quickly distribute our offensive power into more ships.

Stalking the marble halls of Washington are men who have a phobia against aircraft carriers. Let them not misconstrue the meaning of missile chess. Missile chess is not a parable against sea-based air power; it is a parable in favor of a balanced battle fleet. To *remove* sea-based aviation would be to remove the queen. Let us set aside the parable and speak plainly about a balanced fleet on its merits. It is a force which might have its offensive power distributed roughly as follows.

Such a battle force will continue to have as its nucleus one or more carriers, the number driven by the extent of the threat in the offing and the tactical circumstances. Smaller carriers in greater numbers would be pleasant to contemplate, but the facts are that economies of scale drive carrier efficiency, and given that the carriers can be reasonably safeguarded, bigger ships offer disproportionately greater combat strength. Carrier aircraft with their awesome range and power of repeated strikes have no rival for sustaining the attack.

But the enemy (which, in these days of first-rate technology in the hands of second-rate countries, need not be the Soviet Union) cannot be allowed to believe it is home free if it incapacitates one or two ships. Therefore, we should add Harpoon- and Tomahawk-carrying missile ships in numbers of, perhaps, six per carrier. These ships, being numerous, must be inexpensive, if $100–200 million can be thought of as inexpensive. They cannot be expected to have much more defensive armament than point defense. They depend for their survival on the carriers' fighters, on yet-to-be-described antiair warfare missile-armed ships (AAW), and, one would hope, on active and passive electronic countermeasures. In the nature of the war, all will not survive: their role might be likened to the battle fleet's destroyers of the 1920s and 1930s. Their missiles should carry both conventional and nuclear warheads. These new "destroyers" present the enemy with an impossible targeting problem. They have no sustained firepower, yet they threaten to survive a surprise attack from the sea and assure a devastating counterattack; to present a massive nuclear retaliatory threat to the enemy ashore; or to pave the way for carrier air power by nonnuclear precision first strikes on airfields and command and control centers. Like pawns on a chessboard, individually their offensive capacity is limited, but collectively they are a powerful, threatening force.

Third, there should be ships with Aegis and other surface-to-air missile ships, three or four or more per battle group, depending again on the mission and the threat. In the narrow sense, the AAW missile ships defend the carriers. In a broader sense, their purpose is to present the enemy with an insoluble dilemma. If the opposing fleet tries to take out the AAW ships first, our battle force's offensive missile ships and attack aircraft will destroy it. If the enemy aims at the carrier and the "destroyers," the Aegis ship and her companions will survive to forestall the missile threat. The AAW missile ships, like knights and bishops, will absorb attacks that would otherwise fall upon the queen.

The fourth component of the future battle force comprises attack submarines in direct support. Armed with missiles, increasingly they should be appreciated as much as an offensive component of battle force combat power as they are as a defensive component. They heighten the discomfort of the enemy in the same way the hypothetical destroyers do. Their roles are verisimilitudinous to destroyers in the sense that the former are more survivable and freer to roam the seas, but the latter are much cheaper per weapon carried and more easily commanded.

Finally, let us remove the battle force commander from the carrier. It sounds inefficient to build a ship the foremost purpose of which is to carry the officer in tactical command. But when the added complication imposed on the enemy of having to deal with a *fifth* kind of target is appreciated, then a specialized flagship makes sense. Our five battle force components each in a different way will be imperative targets for immediate destruction. The enemy is presented with an impossible coordination problem. Nor is it any longer axiomatic that the officer in tactical command can command best from his carrier. In this balanced force the offensive capability is dispersed throughout the force. If the carriers are lost, the battle may be *lost*, but it is folly to think that the battle will be *over*. The king should not be chained to his queen.

Here, then, are five components of a battle force whose offensive power is distributed and balanced. We have not entered explicitly into the antisubmarine warfare question. Suffice to say in passing that the concept of spreading the offense for the sake of survivability against air and surface missiles will serve as well to dilute the threat from submarine-launched missiles.

Having constructed a new battle force, let us evaluate it in three sets of circumstances. The first is the bread-and-butter mission: to project power in a war in which the Soviet Union is passive. As before, the carriers will move in to project their formidable, sustained, striking power. The other components are largely extraneous, with the officer in tactical command back in his carrier, submarines detached, surface combatants few in numbers, and logistics support ships the tail that may wag the dog. But this comfortable pattern of operations is obsolescent. Increasingly our prospective antagonists, in the Middle East, for example, will be well armed with some share of sophisticated weaponry. Soviet forces may be present, and they, unlike heretofore, cannot be discounted or ignored. Therefore, in many if not most crisis or limited war situations, elements of the other four battle fleet components—guided missile cruisers, destroyers, attack submarines, and a flagship—will be needed. In old-fashioned terms, we should sacrifice some efficiency in *power projection* for the sake of *sea control*.

Second, the battle force must deal with a localized direct confrontation with the Soviet Union itself: Black's pieces painted Red. Mark how that over the course of the last decade changes have taken place. It is reasonable to imagine circumstances in which we may be outnumbered by Soviet naval forces on scene. This is no time to be confronting a Red Navy with only one or two ships that can hurt it. The Soviets must know that if they attack they will assuredly suffer and may lose. In addition, Red naval forces are configured for nuclear attack. Ours are not. The change—the new element—is that the United States no longer has strategic weapon superiority. A fundamental shift occurred when the Soviets became free to contemplate a theater nuclear attack in an atmosphere of strategic parity. If there is such a thing as a theater nuclear war that can be contained, then it is most likely to occur at sea, simply because vital national interests will be *less* threatened and the homeland will not have been struck. Likely or not, the temptation to the Soviets will be to redress their naval conventional weapon inferiority with their nuclear weapon superiority. The way to reduce the temptation is to eliminate the asymmetry, by spreading an offensive nuclear weapon capability through our battle groups.

Finally, there is the mission of deterring a major war with the Soviet Union. The battle fleet helps deter today by posing a substantive conventional weapon threat to the Soviet homeland. One should not view its potential as hollow on grounds that the war would escalate into a nuclear exchange. One should view the U.S. battle fleet as helping to dissuade the Soviets from starting and winning a war without nuclear weapons because we have no conventional response. Our conventional naval offensive power has a value we should cherish. To put its value in perspective, it is well to consider how the peacetime battle fleet has paid for itself by evoking a massive response on the part of the Soviet Union. Contrary to those who argue that the battle fleet engenders a naval arms race, our carrier battle groups have diverted resources that could otherwise have been devoted to the Red Army and Air Force.

Since the end of World War II, the Red Navy has been charged with, and frustrated in, its responsibility to defend the Soviet homeland against our carrier striking power and our strategic submarines. For them, defending against the threat of the U.S. Navy has been a running sore, involving many false starts and the expenditure of vast resources at less payoff than the United States has had in return for our substantial naval investments. Because of the U.S. Navy, Soviet naval strategy has been focused on defense. Sobering indeed is a moment or two of reflection on what would be the potential of their navy to cut off our military reinforcement to NATO, hazard the very ingress and egress of our ballistic missile submarines, interdict and harass our economic trade partners the mere symbol of which is Saudi Arabia, and without firing a shot create untoward mischief anywhere in the world, all of which would befall if there were no deployed battle groups.

Our suspicion must be, moreover, that offensive power represented exclusively by our 13 carriers is a problem the Soviets now have nearly solved. There should be few more important national military objectives than to raise the specter again of the power of our Navy to inflict mighty damage on the Soviet homeland. The way to accomplish this is to distribute our striking power more evenly through the ships of the fleet.

The burden of this essay is that the circumstances under which naval battles will be fought are rapidly changing, that the U.S. Navy's offensive power is over-concentrated in a small number of ships, and that we are not adapting quickly enough to these new circumstances. But the essay is not the parable of naval conflict. The *parable* lies in *playing* missile chess. There is a vividness that emerges from the play of the game that words cannot describe. How the asymmetry in firepower leads White and Black to dissimilar tactics. How both sides suffer from a prospective shortage of weapons and must constantly decide whether to capture or wait for a better, or more critical, opportunity, an opportunity which, sometimes, comes too late. How the knights and bishops not only capture, but threaten and distract, and sell themselves dearly in exchange for missiles that the enemy can ill afford to lose. And how, in the end, White's queen and rooks will sweep the chessboard clear if they survive, and of Black's all-consuming search for ways to keep this from happening.

Of course, missile chess is just a game. Chess in comparison with the powerful analogical tools at modern man's disposal for the simulation of war must, in the end, be treated as a bit of whimsy. You are advised to embrace missile chess as mere diversion. If the play insinuates something more: inferences, perhaps, that cannot be shaken . . . reflections . . . conclusions that no simple game on 64 squares can possibly justify . . . if these things come to pass, well, you have been warned.

Note

1. In *Through the Looking Glass*, written by Lewis Carroll, the kings, queens, and knights that Alice encountered were White and Red. The simile between Red and the U.S. Navy's most capable competitor is almost irresistible, but we will stay with White and Black, not just because that is modern chess convention, but especially to emphasize that the U.S. Navy has commitments that extend beyond confronting the Soviet Union.

INDEX

AAW (antiair warfare) missile-armed
ships, 186–87
admiralship, 94, 97, 101–2
Aegean, Battle of the, 2–3, 6–33
air combat tactics: coastal combat
tactical role of, 8; combat role of,
ix; fictional Battle of the Aegean,
10–11; technology and, xi
air superiority and amphibious operations, 154
aircraft: duels between single combatants, ix–x; for Marines, 176–77
aircraft carriers: effects of missile
warfare on, 181, 184–89; fictional
Battle of the Aegean, 14, 19, 21, 23;
importance of to naval tactics, 183;
limits on use of carrier aviation, 3;
for Marines, 176–77, 178; offensive
power of, 184–89; phobia against,
185; procedures on board, 177;
smaller carriers, 186; tactical development for, 52; tactical formations,
35, 130; World War II war plans,
171–72
Aircraft in Warfare (Lanchester), 77
Alacrity (Great Britain), 41–42, 43
Albemarle, x, 77, 78–79

Alliance, 84
Alligator amphibious tractor, 173,
177–78
Ambuscade (Great Britain), 35, 41, 44
"American Naval Policy" (Fiske),
90–111
amphibious command ship, 176
amphibious operations: air superiority
and, 154; amphibious ships, 163–64;
anti-landing defense, 149–65; anti-
landing defense, characteristics of,
150–51; casualty rates, 157–58;
command relationships, unity of
command, and unity of effort, 150,
152–53, 176; defending against
compared to conducting, 145, 149,
164–65; delays and timing of landings, 158–59; doctrine for, 155, 166,
168–80; evolution of, 166; exercises
to test tactics and equipment, 170,
173, 174–76, 177–78; fictional
Battle of the Aegean, 14–15, 16;
force ratios, 156–57; goal of, 3;
Inchon landing, 145–46, 147–49,
154, 155, 158; joint operations,
151–52; landing craft for, 148–49,
161, 170–71, 172–73, 177–78, 179;

undeveloped state of, 101–2; undeveloped state of, reasons for, 102–5; vagueness of, 102

Naval War College: correlation of training of North Atlantic Squadron with work at, 86–87, 88; establishment of, 81, 82, 84, 85; location of, selection of, 85; Luce role at, 81, 82, 84, 85; Mahan role at, 80–81, 82, 87; North Atlantic Squadron and formation tactics development and training, 83–89; professionalization of officer corps and, 82; strategic gaming at, 4, 5–6; tactical development and training purpose of, 81, 82–83

Navy, U.S.: conflict between Marine Corps and, 170–72, 180; imaginary Second Battle of the Nile against Soviets, 1–2; Marine Corps and changes to, 169, 179; Marine Corps commitment to, 179–80; mental work required of officers, 103; morale in, 106; Navy–Marine Corps operations, 166–80; offensive power of carriers, 184–89; officer responsibilities, 103–4; procedures on board ships, 177; professionalization of officer corps, 82; rebuilding a strong fleet, 81; sea power of, 81; strong navy, support for, 81

Nelson, Horatio, 53, 73

network-centric warfare, combat system for, 7

Nevada, 114

New York State Maritime School, 82

night battles, 63, 71–75

Nile, Battle of the, 1–2

Nimitz, Chester W.: Battle of Midway role, 112–28; opinions about, 117–18; staying ashore for command and communication, 29–30

North, Ian, 39–40, 41–43

North Atlantic Squadron: Cooper command of, 84, 88; correlation of training on with work at Naval War College, 86–87, 88; fleet and single combat unit, identity of squadron as, 86–87, 88; formation tactics development and training to support Naval War College, 83–89; Jouett command of, 85, 88–89; Luce command of, 84–85, 88–89; Luce service in, 82; scattering of ships for duties, 82, 86–87; ships assigned to, 84, 85–86; southern ports, tour to, 85–86; training plan and exercises, 88–89

nuclear weapons: development and use of, 58; Korean War and consideration to use, 160; nuclear warfare tactics, x; strategic weapons, handling of in battle, x

O'Brian, Patrick, 76

O'Hare, Butch, 76–77

O'Kane, Dick, 77

Oklahoma, 114

Oliver Hazard Perry–class frigates, 141, 143

One Hundred Days (Woodward), 34–46

operational art (campaign planning), xi

original ideas, proposal of, 135

Ossipee, 88

overwhelming force, 157

peacetime tactical development and readiness, xi, 55–56, 59–61, 107–11, 182–83

Pensacola, 86

people, importance of to defense of country, 61

Peres, Shimon, 65–66

ABOUT THE EDITOR

Captain Wayne P. Hughes graduated from the U.S. Naval Academy in 1952. He commanded the USS *Hummingbird* (MSC 192) and USS *Morton* (DD 948) and served three tours in the Korean and Vietnam War zones. He has a master of science degree in operations research and taught U.S. foreign policy and naval history at the Naval Academy. Among his several operations analysis tours, he was deputy director of Systems Analysis (Op-96). Since then, he has served as chief of naval education and training support and executive assistant and naval aide to the undersecretary of the Navy. Hughes is the author of the books *Fleet Tactics and Coastal Combat* and *Military Modeling for Decision Making*, the co-author of A *Concise Theory of Combat*, the co-editor of the U.S. Naval Institute's *Classics of Sea Power* series, and the author of numerous articles on naval history, logistics, tactics, and strategy. He now is at the Naval Postgraduate School, where he has held two research chairs, served as dean of the Graduate School of Operations and Information Sciences, and taught naval tactics and campaign analysis.

The Naval Institute Press is the book-publishing arm of the U.S. Naval Institute, a private, nonprofit, membership society for sea service professionals and others who share an interest in naval and maritime affairs. Established in 1873 at the U.S. Naval Academy in Annapolis, Maryland, where its offices remain today, the Naval Institute has members worldwide.

Members of the Naval Institute support the education programs of the society and receive the influential monthly magazine *Proceedings* or the colorful bimonthly magazine *Naval History* and discounts on fine nautical prints and on ship and aircraft photos. They also have access to the transcripts of the Institute's Oral History Program and get discounted admission to any of the Institute-sponsored seminars offered around the country.

The Naval Institute's book-publishing program, begun in 1898 with basic guides to naval practices, has broadened its scope to include books of more general interest. Now the Naval Institute Press publishes about seventy titles each year, ranging from how-to books on boating and navigation to battle histories, biographies, ship and aircraft guides, and novels. Institute members receive significant discounts on the Press's more than eight hundred books in print.

Full-time students are eligible for special half-price membership rates. Life memberships are also available.

For a free catalog describing Naval Institute Press books currently available, and for further information about joining the U.S. Naval Institute, please write to:

Member Services
U.S. NAVAL INSTITUTE
291 Wood Road
Annapolis, MD 21402-5034
Telephone: (800) 233-8764
Fax: (410) 571-1703
Web address: www.usni.org